Statistical Methods
for
Environmental Mixtures

Andrea Bellavia

Contents

Preface

This book presents an extended version of the material for the winter class in "Statistical methods for Environmental Mixtures" that I taught at the Department of Environmental Health, Harvard T.H. Chan School of Public Health (HSPH), between 2018 and 2020. The course was designed as a 2-weeks intensive introductory class, which made it realistically impossible to cover all topics and methodologies related to the rapidly expanding field of statistical approaches for high-dimensional exposures and their application in exposome research. As such, the goal of this document is not to comprehensibly summarize the existing literature, but rather to introduce the rational and importance of evaluating environmental exposures as mixtures, to present selected topics within the field, and to provide illustrative examples and critical discussion. The content of the course was designed for students and researchers in environmental health sciences with limited statistical background, and this teaching format has been maintained in this book.

Credits should also go to Dr. Paige Williams and Prof. Brent Coull (from the Department of Biostatistic at HSPH) who gave guest lectures on principal components analysis and Bayesian Kernel Machine Regression during the course: the sections on these topics are largely taken from the material they shared and presented. A special thanks also goes to Dr. Stefano Renzetti (University of Brescia) who shared relevant material on weighted quantile sum regression.

The R statistical software was used for the practical sessions in class. Despite some introduction to the specific packages and code examples are here provided, the reader should refer to online documentations, provided at various links throughout the book, for detailed descriptions of the software.

About the Author

Andrea Bellavia, PhD, is a biostatistician currently located in Boston, MA. From 2016 to 2020 he has served as instructor and research scientist at the Harvard T.H. Chan School of Public Health in the departments of Environmental Health and Biostatistics. He has led and coauthored more than 50 scientific publications mainly focusing on the development and application of statistical methods for high-dimensional exposures, time-to-event analysis, and mediation and interaction analysis.

Webpage: https://andreabellavia.github.io

The author takes full responsibility for the content of this book. Figures and Tables from published papers are included upon journals' permissions.

Cover art by Maria Bellavia

Chapter 1

Introduction

A major goal of public health research is the study of the complex mechanisms leading to the development of diseases in humans, and the identification of potentially modifiable risk factors that could be targeted to reduce the burden of diseases in the overall population or in specific subgroups at high risk. A considerable number of potentially modifiable risk factors have been thoroughly studied, including dietary constituents, environmental factors such as chemicals and pollutants, lifestyle, social, and other ecological factors. Nevertheless, throughout their lifetime, humans are exposed to hundreds of these factors, which jointly contribute to the development of a given disease with complex mechanisms that can also involve antagonistic or synergistic interactions. This complex set of exposure is commonly referred to as "exposome" (Vermeulen et al. 2020).

Even when restricting our focus on environmental exposures - a substantial component of the exposome - it is recognized that we are simultaneously exposed to hundreds of chemicals and pollutants. For example it has been shown that a given blood or urine sample taken from a random American will contain some concentration of at least 400 different chemicals. A group of 3 or more chemicals/pollutants, simultaneously present in nature or in the human body, is commonly defined as an environmental mixture.

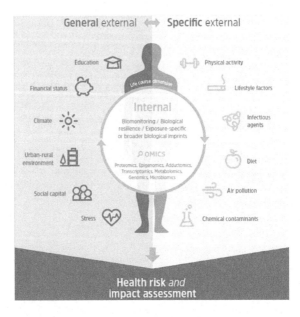

Figure 1.1: The exposome (illustration by Utrecht University)

1.1 Environmental mixtures

Common statistical approaches that have been used on a daily basis in environmental epidemiology might fail to capture the complexity of exposures in our world. For several years, despite recognizing that individuals are commonly exposed to multiple environmental factors, the "one-at-the-time" approach has remained the standard practice in most epidemiologic research. To better understand what we mean by "one-at-the-time" approach, and its limitations, let's think of a study where we want to evaluate the effects of parabens - endocrine disrupting chemicals commonly used in the production of personal care products and cosmetics - on diabetes in a population of 1000 individuals. Let's assume that through urine samples analysis we were able to detect concentrations of three common parabens compounds (metylparaben, butylparaben, propylparaben) in most of our individuals. The "one-at-the-time" approach would build 3 independent statistical models (these could even be very sophisticated models that account for any level of data complexity), one for each parabens compound, adjusting for potential confounders of the associations but without taking into account the other 2 detected compounds. This approach is subject to three main limitations:

- We know that individuals are exposed to multiple factors, and we might want to estimate the joint (also knows as cumulative) effects of these chemicals. A "one-at-the-time" approach does not allow responding to this question.

- Is there any interaction between the three compounds in predicting diabetes? A "one-at-the-time" approach does not allow responding to this question.

- Last but not least, this approach is making strong assumptions with regards to the causal structure underlying the data. Specifically, we are assuming that, very unrealistically, the association between each compound and the outcome is not confounded by the presence of any of the other compounds. The "one-at-the-time"is affected by confounding bias.

To overcome these 3 major limitations we need to evaluate exposure to parabens as a mixture of the three evaluated compounds, building a single statistical model that could jointly evaluate the three exposures and possibly accounting for co-confounding, interactions, and other specific features of the data. Obtaining such statistical model is not easy, and things would only get more complex if we wanted to account for a larger mixture of chemicals, or even to incorporate several groups of exposures in an exposome-wide analysis. Over the last decade or so, many researchers have focused their effort on developing statistical approaches for environmental mixtures, adapting techniques from other fields or developing new methodologies from scratch. The National Institute of Environmental Health Sciences (NIEHS) launched a specific initiative, called Powering Research Through Innovative Methods for Mixtures in Epidemiology (PRIME), to encourage methods developments in this direction, and organized workshops and symposiums on the topics. An important symposium in 2015 identified several available approaches and discussed advantages and limitations for each (Taylor et al. 2016). Five years later the number of available approaches has multiplied, and several of the discussed methodologies have been extended, revised, and presented to the public. The field of environmental epidemiology is gradually moving to a multi-pollutants or multi-chemical framework as a default (Dominici et al. 2010), leading the ground in exposome research, and more and more papers are published every year within this topic.

The goal of this class (and of this book) is to present and discuss some of these approaches, presenting their advantages and limitations and, most importantly, discussing what research question they target and when they should be chosen to evaluate environmental mixtures. While it is impossible to cover all available techniques in a short time, references for alternative methodologies that are not discussed here will be provided. Most of the examples and discussion will focus on environmental exposures; it comes without saying that extension of these approaches into other fields of exposome research (e.g. evaluating multiple nutrients, multiple lifestyle factors ...) is recommended and would provide enormous benefits.

1.2 Research questions of interest

When evaluating a set of environmental factors detected in a given population as an environmental mixture, a critical step is the clarification of the research question of interest. The discussion of the different methodologies presented in the aforementioned NIEHS workshop concluded that we do not have an optimal approach, but that each method performed well under a specific research question. Here are some of the most common questions that we may want to address:

1. Do we have recurrent patterns of exposures?

With several factors at play, it is often of interest to understand whether specific components of the mixture are clustered into smaller subgroups, based on similar characteristics, shared sources, or other features.

2. What is the overall effect of the mixture on a given out-

come?

From our previous example, we may be interested in evaluating the overall effects of parabens exposure on the risk of diabetes. We are not really interested in the specific role of each compound but only on the cumulative effect of the several components.

3. Who are the bad actors? What are the chemical-specific effects within the mixture?

Let's assume that we have identified a potentially harmful effect of our mixture on the outcome of interest, and we therefore want to reduce the levels of exposures in our population. If question 1 has identified common patterns due to shared sources, we could simply target these sources, disregarding the actual effects of these chemicals. Alternatively, we could try to identify which component of the mixture is responsible for the effect observed in question 2. In our parabens example, if we had observed a positive association we may want to further investigate what parabens compounds are driving the association between the mixture and the outcome.

4. Is there any interaction between chemicals in predicting the outcome?

When more than one mixture component contributes to a given mixture-outcome association, it is reasonable to expect that some kind of interaction between the two will be present and we might want to formally identify and estimate the role of these joint interactive effects.

In general, one might have one or more research questions in mind, or simply want to evaluate the mixture in an exploratory way. No matter what, it will always be recommended to explore different techniques and thoroughly compare and validate results using different approaches.

1.3 Broad classifications of statistical approaches

Over the last few years several papers have reviewed the existing literature on statistical methods for mixtures and provide different criteria for their classifications. Among these, two recommended readings are Hamra and Buckley (2018) and Stafoggia et al. (2017). Simple and relevant classification criteria are the following:

1. Supervised vs unsupervised procedures

This first distinction refers to whether or not the mixture is evaluated by taking into account its association with a given outcome of interest. We will discuss in Section 2 that, before evaluating the effects of our exposures on health outcomes, it is important to carefully assess the features of the mixture, especially when this is composed by a high number of components, investigating its correlations structure and identifying the presence of subgroups or clusters of exposures. To this end, we turn to unsupervised techniques that directly focus on characterizing the complex mixture of exposures without any reference to a given outcome of interest such as principal component analysis. Supervised techniques, on the other hand, attempt to account for the complex nature of exposures while investigating a given mixture-outcome association.

2. Data reduction vs variable selection techniques.

The common goal of all approaches that we will discuss is to reduce the complexity of the data to be able to assess mixtures-outcome associations while losing as little information as possible. This is broadly accomplished in two ways: by summarizing the original exposures into fewer covariates, or by selecting targeted elements of the mixture. We can use the term "data reduction approaches" to describe those techniques that reduce the dimension of the mixture by generating new variables (scores, components, indexes ...). On the other hand, methodologies that select specific elements of the mixture that are directly evaluated with respect to the outcome can be defined as "variable selection approaches."

1.4 Introduction to R packages and illustrative example

All methods presented in this book are implemented in the R statistical software. R is a free statistical software environment that allows you to write your own code and packages, sharing them as open sources. For this reason several recently developed approaches for environmental mixtures are only available in R. Most R packages are accompanied by online tutorials and vignettes that describe all features of the library and provide illustrative examples and explanations. We refer to those documents for the technical information of the R packages, and only briefly discuss methods implementation and results interpretation. The following packages will be used:[1]

```
Packages <- c("readxl", "bkmr", "qgraph", "gWQS",
              "qgcomp", "corrplot", "cluster",
              "factoextra","gridExtra","table1",
              "glmnet")
lapply(Packages, library, character.only = TRUE)
```

As an illustrative example a simulated dataset that was developed for the 2015 NIEHS workshop previously mentioned and made publicly available will be used throughout the text. The dataset is available online.[2] The data includes a mixture of 14 continuous exposures, $(X_1 - X_{14})$, a continuous outcome Y, and 3 additional covariates $(Z_1 - Z_3)$.

Chemical concentrations were generated based on the correlation between log-transformed polychlorinated biphenyls (PCB), dioxins, and furans, from NHANES data. Two clusters of highly-correlated covariates were present ($X_3-X_4-X_5$, and $X_{12} - X_{13}$, while low to moderate correlations were simulated between other covariates. Z_1 and Z_2 were simulated based on poverty index and age, both assumed to be confounders of the association. Z_3 was simulated based on gender distribution, and assumed to be an effect modifier. The outcome was generated with the following functions for male and female, respectively:

---

[1]Throughout the book, grey boxes include R code that can be used to replicate the presented results

[2]https://www.niehs.nih.gov/news/events/pastmtg/2015/statistical/index.cfm

$Z_3 = 0 : E[Y] = 3 + 0.05 \cdot X_4 + 0.1 \cdot X_6 + 0.1 \cdot X_{11} + 0.5 \cdot X_{12} + 0.1 \cdot X_{14} + 0.01 \cdot Z_1 + 0.003 \cdot Z_2$

$Z_3 = 1 : E[Y] = 3 + 0.01 \cdot X_1 + 0.05 \cdot X_4 + 0.1 \cdot X_{11} + 0.1 \cdot X_{14} + 0.01 \cdot Z_1 + 0.003 \cdot Z_2 - 0.32 \cdot (Z_3 = 1)$

Thus, for $Z_3 = 0$ only X_4, X_6, X_{11}, X_{12} and X_{14} are positively associated with Y. When $Z_3 = 1$, only X_1, X_4, X_{11} and X_{14} are associated with Y. Interactions between chemicals were not considered.

Chapter 2

Unsupervised analyses

As introduced in the previous section, the term unsupervised analysis refers to that critical analytic phase where we only focus on the exposures, trying to characterize, explain, and describe the complex environmental mixture of interest. This could even be the ultimate goal of the analysis (as a matter of fact, to respond to common questions such as "what are the most common exposures in our populations?" or "can we identify subgroups of exposures that are commonly observed together?" we do not need to account for the outcome. In other settings, this will still be an important preliminary phase that will inform subsequent analytic steps.

Note that the focus of unsupervised analysis in this context is not on understanding biological mechanisms through which chemicals or pollutants operate in the body, but rather a purely epidemiologic one. By attempting to identify clusters of exposures without accounting for the their relationship with a given outcome we are in fact grouping exposures based on features such as population distribution and shared sources rather than based on similar mechanisms of action.

2.1 Data pre-processing

Before getting into the actual analysis of the mixture it is important to carefully assess each component independently. Environmental exposures such as chemicals or pollutants, but also indicators of greenness, noise, or temperature, share important characteristics that should be carefully addressed.

- Skewedness and variance. Exposures are often non-negative and heavily skewed on the right due to the presence of outliers and to the fact that they are strictly non-negative. For this reason, it is usually recommended to log-transform these exposures. Nevertheless, when such operation is taken into account, researchers have to deal with decisions on how to treat eventual zero-values that do not necessarily represent missing data (see third bullet).

- Centering and standardizing exposures. Mixture components tend to have different and difficult-to-compare scales and variability, even within the same family of exposures. Since these exposures will be eventually evaluated together, centering and standardizing the covariates will allow comparability and improve interpretation of statistical findings.

- Zero values. It is relatively common, when evaluating large mixtures of environmental exposures, to encounter one or more covariates with a considerable amount of values equal to 0. How to deal with such zero-values will have important consequences on the implementation and interpretation of statistical approaches for mixtures. The first question to consider is what these zero values represent: specifically, are they "real zeros" (i.e. the individuals had no exposure to a given chemical), or do they represent non-detected values (i.e. the individual had a low level of exposure that we were not able to detect)? In the first case, the values will have to be treated as an actual zero, with important implications for the analysis. In the second case, non-detected values are usually imputed to a predefined value (several approaches are available) and the covariate can be treated as continuous. We will briefly deal with this when talking about zero-inflated covariates in Section 6.

- Missing values. Finally, it is important to evaluate the percentage of missing values for each exposure in our mixture. Most techniques that allow evaluating the joint effect of several covariates, including regression models, will generally require a complete-case analysis. As such, an individual with just one missing values in one of the several mixture components, will be excluded from the whole analyses. If the proportion of missingness is not too high (10-15%), multiple imputation techniques can be used, even though the user should be aware that most advanced methodologies might not be fully integrated withing a multiple implementation procedure. If the percentage of missingness is too high, there is not too much to be done, and we will have to decide whether to give up the covariate (excluding it from the mixture), or reduce the sample size (excluding all individual with missing values on that component)

The dataset used in the illustrative example includes simulated covariates where this pre-processing steps have been already completed (all values are greater than 0, no missing data are present, covariates are log-transformed and standardized).

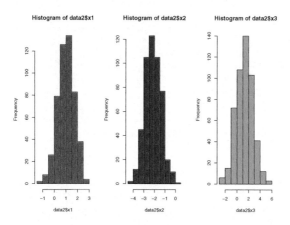

Figure 2.1: Histogram of three mixture components in the simulated data

To conduct a thorough exploratory analysis of environmental mixtures, especially when several covariates are of interest, we encourage the use of the R package `rexposome`.[1]

2.2 Correlation analysis

An essential step in the early phases of a mixture analysis is the assessment of the correlation between mixture components. This preliminary analysis gives a sense of the relationship between exposures, allows a preliminary assessment of exposures patterns and clusters, and gives important information that might inform which method could be better suited for future modeling.

Given two continuous covariates, a simple assessment of their relationship can be checked with a simple two-ways scatterplot. Figure 2.2 shows a set of three 2x2 comparisons, also adding a lowess trend line on top of the scatter plot.

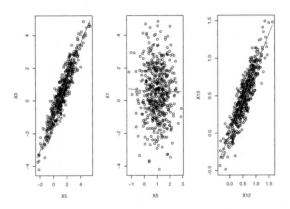

Figure 2.2: Scatter plots of paris of exposures in the simulated data

We see that some combinations of covariates are highly correlated (like X_3 and X_4), while other exposures seem to be completely independent (e.g. X_1 and X_5).

[1]https://www.bioconductor.org/packages/release/bioc/vignettes/rexposome/inst/doc/exposome_data_analysis.html#multivariate-exposome-analysis

A correlation coefficient and a correlation test, will additionally provide a quantitative assessment of this relationship. The Pearson correlation (r) measures the linear dependence between two variables and it can only be used when both covariates are normally distributed:

$$r = \frac{\sum (x - m_x)(y - m_y)}{\sqrt{\sum (x - m_x)^2 (y - m_y)^2}}$$

where m_x and m_y are the means of the two covariates x and y

The Spearman correlation (ρ) measures the correlation between the rank of the two covariates x and y:

$$\rho = \frac{\sum (x' - m_{x'})(y' - m_{y'})}{\sqrt{\sum (x' - m_{x'})^2 (y' - m_{y'})^2}}$$

where $m_{x'}$ and $m_{y'}$ are the ranks of x and y. This correlation test is non-parametric and does not require assuming normality for the two evaluated covariates. Both r and ρ are bounded between -1 and 1 (negative and positive correlation). There is no correlation between the covariates when the coefficient is equal to 0. Tests for significance of the correlation coefficient are available for both r and ρ, testing the null hypothesis of no correlation.

When evaluating the correlation between several exposures we can create a correlation matrix, displayed in Table 2.1. This can be graphically displayed as a correlation plot (or correlogram), which can be plotted using the package corrplot. Note that the command requires the input of the correlation matrix you previously defined.

```
cor.matrix <- cor(data2[,3:16], method="spearman")

corrplot(cor.matrix,
         method="circle",
```

Table 2.1: Correlation matrix from the simulated data

	x1	x2	x3	x4	x5	x6	x7	x8	x9	x10	x11	x12	x13	x14
x1	1.00	0.30	-0.04	-0.03	-0.03	0.04	0.16	-0.05	0.15	-0.10	-0.11	0.35	0.34	0.01
x2	0.30	1.00	0.05	0.06	0.08	0.07	0.18	0.03	0.14	-0.02	-0.03	0.39	0.38	0.05
x3	-0.04	0.05	1.00	0.99	0.93	0.60	0.28	0.74	0.17	0.40	0.56	-0.11	-0.14	0.70
x4	-0.03	0.06	0.99	1.00	0.94	0.61	0.29	0.74	0.18	0.41	0.57	-0.09	-0.13	0.71
x5	-0.03	0.08	0.93	0.94	1.00	0.59	0.29	0.72	0.17	0.42	0.56	-0.10	-0.14	0.69
x6	0.04	0.07	0.60	0.61	0.59	1.00	0.46	0.64	0.38	0.45	0.54	0.06	0.03	0.62
x7	0.16	0.18	0.28	0.29	0.29	0.46	1.00	0.39	0.70	0.36	0.41	0.46	0.48	0.41
x8	-0.05	0.03	0.74	0.74	0.72	0.64	0.39	1.00	0.37	0.55	0.64	0.01	-0.03	0.74
x9	0.15	0.14	0.17	0.18	0.17	0.38	0.70	0.37	1.00	0.32	0.36	0.50	0.50	0.40
x10	-0.10	-0.02	0.40	0.41	0.42	0.45	0.36	0.55	0.32	1.00	0.77	0.00	-0.05	0.42
x11	-0.11	-0.03	0.56	0.57	0.56	0.54	0.41	0.64	0.36	0.77	1.00	-0.01	-0.07	0.54
x12	0.35	0.39	-0.11	-0.09	-0.10	0.06	0.46	0.01	0.50	0.00	-0.01	1.00	0.90	0.11
x13	0.34	0.38	-0.14	-0.13	-0.14	0.03	0.48	-0.03	0.50	-0.05	-0.07	0.90	1.00	0.07
x14	0.01	0.05	0.70	0.71	0.69	0.62	0.41	0.74	0.40	0.42	0.54	0.11	0.07	1.00

```
order = "hclust",
addrect =10,
tl.pos = "l",
tl.col = "black",
sig.level = 0.05)
```

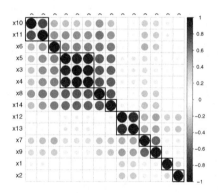

Figure 2.3: Correlation plot from simulated data

A very detailed and useful documentation for the corrplot package is available online.[2]

The correlation plot displayed in Figure 2.3 provides several

[2]https://cran.r-project.org/web/packages/corrplot/vignettes/corrplot-intro.html

important information: first of all, we see a cluster of highly correlated exposures (X_3, X_4, X_5), and a cluster of moderately correlated exposures (X_{12}, X_{13}). In addition, we see that additional pairs of exposures exhibit low to moderate levels of correlation, and it is not straightforward to clearly define additional subgroups of exposures.

2.2.1 Weighted correlation network analysis

Network analysis is emerging as a flexible and powerful technique in different fields. In a nutshell, a network is a complex structure of variables, called nodes, and the relationships (formally called edges) between these nodes. Correlation networks define such relationships on the basis of the quantitative correlations of the nodes, and are increasingly being used in biology to analyze high-dimensional data sets. Weighted correlation networks, in particular, preserve the continuous nature of the underlying correlation information without dicothomizing information. While the theory behind network analysis is beyond the scope of this course, and we refer to other publications for further details (Langfelder and Horvath (2008)), (Hevey (2018)), it is here useful to mention that these networks can be used in descriptive analyses to graphically display the relationship between exposures in our mixture based on the correlation structure. This can be now obtained with several R packages, including `qgraph`, used to derive the plot in Figure 2.4, and `bootnet`.[3]

---

[3] http://sachaepskamp.com/tutorials

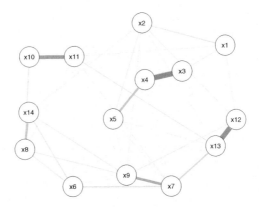

Figure 2.4: Weighted correlation network of exposures in the simulated data

This network confirms our finding from the correlation plot, but provides a different and possibly better way of representing and visualizing the relationships between components of the mixture.

2.3 Principal component analysis

Principal Component Analysis (PCA) is a useful technique for exploratory data analysis, which allows a better visualization of the variability present in a dataset with many variables. This "better visualization" is achieved by transforming a set of covariates into a smaller set of principal components.

A principal component can be thought of as the direction where there is the most variance or, geometrically speaking, where the data is most spread out. In practical terms, to derive the first principal component that describe our mixture, we try to find the straight line that best spreads the data out when it is projected along it, thus explaining the most substantial variance in the data. Figure 2.5 shows the first principal component in a simple setting with only 3 covariates of interest (so that we could graphically represent it).

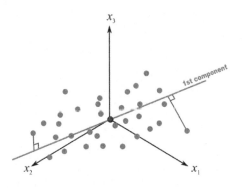

Figure 2.5: First principal component in a 3-covariates setting

Mathematically speaking, this first component t_1 is calculated as a linear combination of the p original predictors $T = XW_p$, where W_p are weights that would maximize the overall explained variability. For those math-oriented readers, it turns out that such weights are the eigenvectors of the correlation matrix of the original exposures.

Once a first component has been retrieved, we proceed by calculating a second component that would maximize the residual variance. Of interest in our context, the procedure adds a constraints of orthogonality to this second component, that is, it will be uncorrelated to the first one, as presented in Figure 2.6.

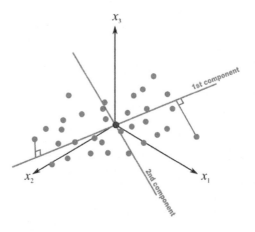

Figure 2.6: Second principal component in a 3-covariates setting

Mathematically, this is obtained by another linear combination where the weights are the eigenvectors corresponding to the second largest eigenvalue. In this way we can proceed to derive a full set of p components from our original p covariates, until all variance has been explained. In summary, PCA is a set of linear transformation that fits the matrix of exposures into a new coordinate system so that the most variance is explained by the first coordinate, and each subsequent coordinate is orthogonal to the last and has a lesser variance. Practically, we are transforming a set of p correlated variables into a set of p uncorrelated principal components. PCA is sensitive to unscaled covariates, so it is usually recommended to standardize your matrix of exposures before running a PCA analysis.

2.3.1 Fitting a PCA in R

There are several options to conduct PCA in R. Here we will use `prcomp` but alternative options are available (`princomp` and `principal`). PCA is also available in the aforementioned `rexposome` package. To prepare nice figures for presentations or usage in manuscripts one could also consider the `factoextra` package, which creates a ggplot2-based elegant visualization.[4]

The `prcomp( )` function produces a basic principal component analysis. The command requires the raw data we want to reduce (the exposure matrix) and will extract principal components. Here we are also centering and scaling all exposures.

```
fit <- prcomp(X, center=TRUE, scale=TRUE)
```

2.3.2   Choosing the number of components

One of the most interesting features of PCA is that, while it is possible to calculate p components from a set of p covariates, we usually need a smaller number to successfully describe most of the variance of the original matrix of exposures. In practical terms, not only we are reshaping the original set of exposures into uncorrelated principal components, but we are also able to reduce the dimension of the original matrix into a smaller number of variables that describe the mixture. How many components do we actually need? Before getting to describe the several tools that can guide us on this decision, it is important to stress that this step will be purely subjective. Sometimes these tools will lead to the same evident conclusion, but other times it might not be straightforward to identify a clear number of components that describe the original data. In general, the three common tools used to select a number of components include:

- Select components that explain at least 70 to 80% of the original variance
- Select components corresponding to eigenvalues larger than 1
- Look at the point of inflation in the scree plot

Let's take a look at these approaches in our illustrative example. These are the results of the PCA that we ran with the previous R command:

---

[4]http://www.sthda.com/english/wiki/factoextra-r-package-easy-multivariate-data-analyses-and-elegant-visualization

```
summary(fit)

## Importance of components:
##                          PC1    PC2     PC3     PC4
## Standard deviation     2.4627 1.7521 1.12071 0.89784
## Proportion of Variance 0.4332 0.2193 0.08971 0.05758
## Cumulative Proportion  0.4332 0.6525 0.74219 0.79977
##                           PC5     PC6     PC7      P
## Standard deviation     0.83905 0.72337 0.63861 0.602
## Proportion of Variance 0.05029 0.03738 0.02913 0.025
## Cumulative Proportion  0.85006 0.88744 0.91657 0.942
##                          PC9    PC10    PC11    PC1
## Standard deviation     0.4892 0.46054 0.43573 0.2975
## Proportion of Variance 0.0171 0.01515 0.01356 0.0063
## Cumulative Proportion  0.9596 0.97476 0.98832 0.9946
##                          PC13    PC14
## Standard deviation     0.25542 0.09904
## Proportion of Variance 0.00466 0.00070
## Cumulative Proportion  0.99930 1.00000
```

(Square roots of) eigenvalues are reported in the first line, while the second and third lines present, respectively, the proportion of variance explained by each given component (note that, as expected, this decreases as we proceed with the estimation), and the cumulative variance explained.

The scree plot is the plot of the descending eigenvalues. Ideally we would like to identify a point of inflation (also known as "elbow" of the curve), signifying that after a certain number of components, the proportion of variance that is additionally explained becomes minimal.

```
plot(fit,type="lines")
```

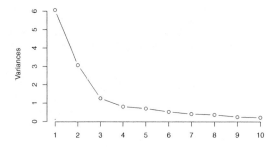

Figure 2.7: Scree plot from simulated dataset

All these techniques seem to indicate that 3 components might successfully describe the original set of 14 exposures.

2.3.3 Getting sense of components interpretation

A PCA is composed by three steps. Fitting the model is the easiest part as it only requires a line of coding (assuming that the pre-processing has been carefully conducted). The second step, selecting the number of components, requires some levels of subjectivity but is also relatively simple in most settings. The third step is usually the more complicated one, as we are now tasked with providing some interpretation to the set of principal components that we have selected. To get a sense of what principal components represent, we usually look at loading factors, the correlation coefficients between the derived components and the original covariates. In practical terms they inform us on how much of the original variance of each covariate is explained by each component. Loading factors for the illustrative example are presented in Table 2.2. It is not simple to identify any clear pattern, as loading factors are generally low, and several covariates seem to equally load to more components. However, there is a trick that can be tried out to improve the interpretation of the components, consisting in rotating the axes. The most common approach to do that is called "varimax."

Table 2.2: Loading factors

	PC1	PC2	PC3	PC4	PC5	PC6	PC7	PC8	PC9	PC10	PC11	PC12	PC13	PC14
x1	0.00	0.30	0.36	0.43	0.77	0.02	-0.06	0.04	0.01	-0.01	0.01	-0.01	0.00	-0.01
x2	0.03	0.28	0.47	0.45	-0.58	-0.35	-0.03	0.20	0.03	-0.04	0.00	-0.01	0.02	0.00
x3	0.36	-0.14	0.27	-0.13	-0.03	0.16	-0.21	-0.09	-0.13	-0.02	-0.06	-0.10	0.45	-0.67
x4	0.36	-0.13	0.28	-0.12	-0.02	0.16	-0.20	-0.10	-0.13	-0.02	-0.05	-0.08	0.33	0.74
x5	0.35	-0.13	0.28	-0.10	-0.04	0.14	-0.22	-0.10	-0.11	-0.02	-0.08	0.15	-0.80	-0.07
x6	0.31	0.01	-0.03	-0.06	0.12	-0.62	0.44	-0.50	-0.22	-0.02	-0.06	-0.01	0.00	-0.01
x7	0.24	0.33	-0.24	-0.14	0.03	-0.28	-0.53	-0.19	0.60	0.05	0.02	0.12	0.04	0.01
x8	0.36	-0.05	-0.01	-0.01	0.03	0.02	0.25	0.32	0.13	0.78	0.27	-0.01	-0.02	0.00
x9	0.20	0.35	-0.31	-0.18	0.08	-0.22	-0.24	0.51	-0.57	-0.08	-0.07	-0.03	-0.02	0.01
x10	0.27	-0.02	-0.41	0.53	-0.09	0.23	0.04	-0.08	0.01	0.11	-0.63	-0.04	0.01	0.00
x11	0.32	-0.05	-0.31	0.39	-0.06	0.18	-0.01	-0.10	-0.07	-0.34	0.70	-0.02	-0.01	-0.01
x12	0.03	0.52	0.04	-0.12	-0.12	0.36	0.24	-0.19	-0.12	0.04	0.02	0.67	0.12	-0.01
x13	0.01	0.53	0.02	-0.17	-0.12	0.29	0.14	-0.23	0.01	0.05	0.03	-0.71	-0.14	-0.01
x14	0.34	0.02	0.06	-0.20	0.07	0.05	0.44	0.43	0.43	-0.50	-0.15	-0.01	0.00	0.00

Let's take a look at the rotated loading factors for the first three components (the ones that we have selected) in our example:

```
rawLoadings_3<-fit$rotation[,1:3]
rotatedLoadings_3<-varimax(rawLoadings_3)$loadings
rotatedLoadings_3
```

```
##
## Loadings:
##        PC1    PC2    PC3
## x1            0.162  0.428
## x2     0.163  0.123  0.506
## x3     0.452 -0.102
## x4     0.455
## x5     0.450
## x6     0.275  0.105 -0.115
## x7            0.435 -0.152
## x8     0.332        -0.131
## x9            0.473 -0.198
## x10           0.178 -0.446
## x11    0.182  0.134 -0.382
## x12           0.466  0.227
## x13           0.473  0.218
## x14    0.332
##
##                   PC1    PC2    PC3
## SS loadings      1.000  1.000  1.000
```

28

```
## Proportion Var 0.071 0.071 0.071
## Cumulative Var 0.071 0.143 0.214
```

Interpretation remains a bit tricky and very subjective, but it definitely improves. With three rotated components we observe covariates groupings that recall what we observed in the network analysis: we have X_1, X_2 with higher loading on PC3, X_7, X_9, X_{12}, X_{13} loading on PC2, and all other exposures loading on PC1.

2.3.4 Using principal components in subsequent analyses

We have here discussed PCA as an unsupervised technique for describing the mixture. Principal components, however, can be used in further analysis, for example including the selected components into a regression model instead of the original exposures. This approach is very appealing in the context of environmental mixtures as it would result into incorporating most of the information of our exposure matrix into a regression models by using uncorrelated covariates, thus overcoming one of the major limitations of using multiple regression in this context (see Section 3). Nevertheless, the validity of this approach is strictly dependent on whether a good interpretation of the components has been determined; in our example we would not conclude that the PCA clearly summarizes exposures into well defined groups, and we would get negligible advantages by including such components into a regression model. The next subsection will present some published papers that applied this technique in environmental epidemiology. On a final note, if subgroups of exposures are clearly identified from a PCA, this information can be incorporated into subsequent modeling technique that will be discussed later.

2.3.5 PCA in practice

Despite several techniques developed ad-hoc for the analysis of environmental mixtures have emerged, PCA remains a very common choice among environmental epidemiologists. Most of the times, the method is used to reduce the dimension of a mixture of correlated exposures into a subset of uncorrelated components that are later included in regression analysis.

As a first example, let's consider a paper by Lee et al. (2017) evaluating the association between pregnancy exposure to 28 contaminants (metals, pesticides, PCBs, phthalates, PFAS, BPA) and socio-economic status in the MIREC study. To summarize the mixture, the Authors conduct a PCA that suggests selecting 11 principal components (Table 5 in the manuscript). Nevertheless, the interpretation of these components is not straightforward (the paper does not mention whether a rotation was considered). The first component has higher loading on PCBs, while the second component has high loading on DEHP metabolites. All other components have high loading on specific subsets of exposures, but fail to uniquely identify clusters of exposures within the mixture. For example, to describe exposure to organochlorine pesticides, the Authors obtain similar loading factors in PC1, PC5, and PC9. Similarly, organophosphate pesticides equivalently load on PC3, PC4, and PC6. As described in the previous paragraphs, this has relevant implications when attempting to evaluate PCA components in a regression model.

Results from the paper indicate that PCBs are associated with the outcome of interest (as they load on PC1), but it is not easy to draw any conclusion about other sets of exposures whose variability is captured by multiple components. To conclude, the real information that a PCA model is giving us in this example is that the mixture is very complex and we do not observe clearly defined subgroups of exposures based on the correlation structure. In such setting, a PCA analysis might not be the best option to evaluate exposure-outcome associations, and other methods should be considered.

A second interesting example can be found in Sanchez et al. (2018), evaluating metals and socio-demographic characteristics in the HEALS study in Bangladesh. Out of a mixture of 15 metals, a rotated PCA identified 6 principal components explaining 81% of the total variability. Differently from the previous examples, such components better identify subgroups of exposures (Table 2 from the manuscript). If we look at these loading factors by row, we see that each metal has a high loading factor with one component, and low loading to all others. For example arsenic is described by PC3, cadmium by PC6, and so on down to zinc, described by PC5. In this situation, a regression model that includes the principal components will have a better interpretation; for example, associations between PC3 and the outcome can be used to retrieve information on the joint associations between arsenic, molybdenum, and tungsten, on the outcome.

Nevertheless, it is important to note some critical limitations of this approach, that remain valid also when a perfect interpretation can be provided. Let's think of this third principal component that is well describing the variability of arsenic, molybdenum, and tungsten. A regression coefficient linking PC3 with the outcome would only tell us how the subgroup of these 3 exposures is associated with the outcome, but would not inform us on which of the three is driving the association, whether all three exposures have effects in the same direction, nor whether there is any interaction between the three components. Moreover, let's not forget that components are calculated as linear combinations of the exposures and without taking the relationship with the outcome into account.

For these reasons, we can conclude that PCA is very powerful tool to be considered in the preliminary unsupervised assessment of the mixture as it can inform subsequent analyses. On the other hand, using derived components into regression modeling must be done with caution, and is usually outperformed by most supervised approaches that we will describe later.

Finally, it is important to mention that several extensions of the classical PCA have been developed, including a supervised version of the approach. These techniques, however, were developed in other fields and have not gained too much popularity in the context of environmental exposures, where alternative supervised approaches, presented in the following sections, are generally used.

2.4 Cluster analysis

While a principal components analysis can be seen as a way to identify subgroups of exposures (the columns of the mixture matrix) within the mixture based on their correlation structure, another useful exploratory analysis consists in identifying subgroups of individuals (the rows of the data) that share similar exposure profiles. This is commonly done with cluster analysis. Like PCA, cluster analysis requires complete data and standardized variables. To group individuals, a distance measure must be identified, with several options available from standard euclidean distance to distances based on the correlations structure.

2.4.1 K-means clustering

The most common approach to partition the data into clusters is an unsupervised approach called k-means clustering. This method classifies objects in k groups (i.e., clusters), so that individuals within the same cluster are as similar as possible, while individuals from different clusters are as dissimilar as possible. To achieve that, clusters are defined in a way that minimizes within-cluster variation. A simple algorithm for k-clustering proceeds as follows:

1. Pre-specify k, the number of clusters
2. Select k random individuals as center for each cluster and define the centroids, vectors of length p that contain the means of all variables for the observation in the cluster. In our context, the p variables are the components of our mixture of interest
3. Define a distance measure. The standard choice is the euclidean distance defined as $(x_i - \mu_k)$ i, for each individual in the study (x_i) and each cluster center (μ_k)
4. Assign each individual to the closest centroid
5. For each of the k clusters update the cluster centroid by calculating the new mean values of all the data points in the cluster
6. Iteratively update the previous 2 steps until the the cluster assignments stop changing or the maximum number of iterations is reached. By default, the R software uses

10 as the default value for the maximum number of iterations

This simple algorithm minimizes the total within-cluster variation, defined for each cluster C_k as the sum of squared euclidean distances within that cluster $W(C_k) = \sum_{x_i \in C_k} (x_i - \mu_k)^2$.

Since k-mean clustering requires the user to specify the number of groups, it is important to assess the optimal number of groups. A simple technique is to use the elbow method, similar to the one presented for PCA, which consists in plotting the within-cluster sum of squares versus the number of clusters, and locating the bend in the plot.

2.4.2 K-means in R

We can compute k-means in R with the `kmeans` function within the `cluster` package. Here we are selecting 3 groups, also using the `nstart` option that will attempts multiple initial configurations (here 20) and report the best one.

```
k3 <- kmeans(X, centers = 3, nstart = 20)
```

The function `fviz_cluster` provides a nice graphical representation of the groupings. If there are more than two variables `fviz_cluster` will perform principal component analysis (PCA) and plot the data points according to the first two principal components that explain the majority of the variance.

```
fviz_cluster(k3, data = X)
```

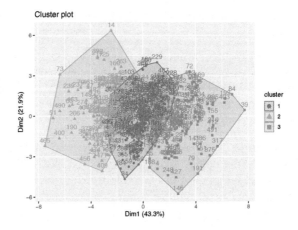

Figure 2.8: Cluster analysis with 3 groups in the simulated data

Here we can test more number of clusters

```
p1 <- fviz_cluster(k2, geom = "point", data = X) +
    ggtitle("k = 2")
p2 <- fviz_cluster(k3, geom = "point", data = X) +
    ggtitle("k = 3")
p3 <- fviz_cluster(k4, geom = "point", data = X) +
    ggtitle("k = 4")
p4 <- fviz_cluster(k5, geom = "point", data = X) +
    ggtitle("k = 5")

grid.arrange(p1, p2, p3, p4, nrow = 2)
```

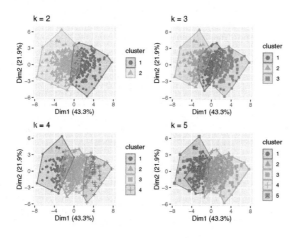

Figure 2.9: Cluster analysis with 2-5 groups

The elbow plot (Figure 2.10) can tell us how many groups optimally classify individuals, showing here that 2 clusters might be enough.

```
set.seed(123)
fviz_nbclust(X, kmeans, method = "wss")
```

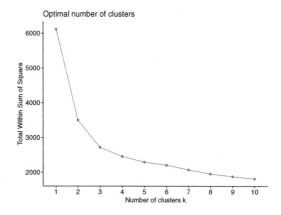

Figure 2.10: Elbow plot from simulated data

2.4.3 Cluster analysis to simplify descriptive statistics presentation

One of the advantages of clustering individuals is to provide a better presentation of descriptive statistics and univariate associations with other covariates in the dataset prior to formal analysis (what is commonly done in table 1 of a scientific manuscript). First, let's define the exposure profiles by evaluating the distribution of original exposures in the clusters (Table 2.3).

We see that individuals in the first cluster have higher exposure levels to most of the included contaminants, so we could define cluster 1 as "high" and cluster 2 as "low" exposure. Next, we can use the clusters to assess the distribution of outcome and covariates by clustering (Table 2.4).

We see that both $z1$, $z2$, $z3$, as well as the outcome are higher among individuals in cluster 1, who are characterized by the exposure profile presented in the previous table.

Table 2.3: Exposure distributions by clusters in the simulated data

	1	2	Overall
	(N=236)	(N=264)	(N=500)
x1			
Mean (SD)	1.04 (0.718)	1.01 (0.684)	1.02 (0.699)
Median [Min, Max]	1.04 [-1.18, 2.49]	1.02 [-0.936, 2.89]	1.03 [-1.18, 2.89]
x2			
Mean (SD)	-2.05 (0.765)	-2.18 (0.759)	-2.12 (0.764)
Median [Min, Max]	-2.10 [-4.32, 0.193]	-2.23 [-4.01, -0.291]	-2.14 [-4.32, 0.193]
x3			
Mean (SD)	2.48 (0.885)	0.291 (0.907)	1.32 (1.41)
Median [Min, Max]	2.36 [0.993, 5.43]	0.511 [-2.33, 1.83]	1.33 [-2.33, 5.43]
x4			
Mean (SD)	3.49 (0.867)	1.33 (0.889)	2.35 (1.39)
Median [Min, Max]	3.39 [1.93, 6.36]	1.51 [-1.36, 2.92]	2.32 [-1.36, 6.36]
x5			
Mean (SD)	1.86 (1.03)	-0.645 (1.04)	0.537 (1.62)
Median [Min, Max]	1.81 [-0.311, 4.85]	-0.459 [-4.22, 1.42]	0.504 [-4.22, 4.85]
x6			
Mean (SD)	1.52 (0.892)	0.326 (0.815)	0.891 (1.04)
Median [Min, Max]	1.50 [-0.564, 3.76]	0.356 [-2.12, 2.25]	0.833 [-2.12, 3.76]
x7			
Mean (SD)	1.51 (0.556)	1.15 (0.490)	1.32 (0.552)
Median [Min, Max]	1.51 [0.216, 2.94]	1.18 [-0.356, 2.50]	1.33 [-0.356, 2.94]
x8			
Mean (SD)	3.39 (0.737)	2.08 (0.767)	2.70 (0.999)
Median [Min, Max]	3.31 [1.65, 5.92]	2.10 [-0.268, 4.84]	2.69 [-0.268, 5.92]
x9			
Mean (SD)	1.45 (0.529)	1.21 (0.571)	1.32 (0.564)
Median [Min, Max]	1.43 [0.0496, 2.70]	1.25 [-0.328, 2.98]	1.34 [-0.328, 2.98]
x10			
Mean (SD)	3.46 (0.690)	2.86 (0.683)	3.14 (0.748)
Median [Min, Max]	3.42 [1.69, 5.26]	2.81 [1.07, 4.66]	3.13 [1.07, 5.26]
x11			
Mean (SD)	5.61 (0.638)	4.81 (0.674)	5.19 (0.769)
Median [Min, Max]	5.53 [3.98, 7.80]	4.80 [2.62, 6.71]	5.21 [2.62, 7.80]
x12			
Mean (SD)	0.466 (0.337)	0.493 (0.347)	0.481 (0.342)
Median [Min, Max]	0.443 [-0.429, 1.15]	0.507 [-0.481, 1.49]	0.483 [-0.481, 1.49]
x13			
Mean (SD)	0.530 (0.348)	0.578 (0.348)	0.555 (0.349)
Median [Min, Max]	0.514 [-0.371, 1.42]	0.570 [-0.355, 1.65]	0.552 [-0.371, 1.65]
x14			
Mean (SD)	1.79 (0.549)	0.881 (0.562)	1.31 (0.719)
Median [Min, Max]	1.79 [0.373, 3.55]	0.879 [-1.29, 2.64]	1.31 [-1.29, 3.55]

Table 2.4: Covariate distributions by clusters in the simulated data

	1	2	Overall
	(N=236)	(N=264)	(N=500)
Outcome			
Mean (SD)	4.19 (0.619)	3.64 (0.569)	3.90 (0.653)
Median [Min, Max]	4.17 [2.66, 6.00]	3.62 [2.25, 5.22]	3.87 [2.25, 6.00]
Poverty index			
Mean (SD)	2.26 (1.59)	1.90 (1.63)	2.07 (1.62)
Median [Min, Max]	2.18 [-1.87, 7.62]	1.87 [-2.47, 5.95]	2.08 [-2.47, 7.62]
Age			
Mean (SD)	46.4 (18.8)	14.4 (17.9)	29.5 (24.3)
Median [Min, Max]	45.2 [1.01, 102]	15.1 [-38.3, 54.3]	28.6 [-38.3, 102]

Chapter 3

Regression-based approaches

The previous section described a set of unsupervised techniques for the analysis of environmental mixtures. These are used to process the complex data before further analyses and to address well defined research questions related to the identification of common patterns of exposures or clustering of individuals based on exposure profiles. In the context of environmental health studies, however, the ultimate goal is often to investigate whether exposure to mixtures of environmental factors are associated with a given health outcome, and possibly whether these associations represent causal effects. Epidemiologists are usually trained to address these questions using regression-based techniques such as generalized linear models, for binary and continuous outcomes, or parametric and semi-parametric regression techniques for survival data, for time-to-event outcomes. Nevertheless, environmental exposures often present complex settings that require handling regression with care. The goal of this section is to present the use of classical regression techniques (i.e. ordinary least squares (OLS)) in mixtures modeling, describe its limitations, and introduce some important extensions of OLS that allow overcoming these shortcomings.

3.1 Ordinary Least Squares (OLS) regression

3.1.1 Chemical-specific regression (EWAS)

A simple way to assess the association between a set of p environmental exposures $(X_1 - X_p)$ and a given outcome Y is to build p different regression models, one for each exposure (the approach that we previously described as "one-at-the-time"). Each model can be further adjusted for potential confounders of each exposure-outcome association. For example, is Y was a continuous exposure, we could fit a set of linear regression models such as: $E[Y|X_1, C] = \beta_0 + \beta_1 \cdot X_1 + \beta \cdot C$. The implicit assumption of this modeling procedure is that, for each element of the mixture, the other components do not act as confounders of the exposure-outcome association, as depicted in the Directed Acyclic Graph (DAG) presented in Figure 3.1.

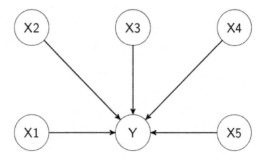

Figure 3.1: DAG for five mixture components independently associated with the outcome

When evaluating a set of environmental exposures, this procedure of fitting a set of independent regression models is usually referred to as environment-wide association study (EWAS, Patel et al. 2010). This approach usually requires correcting for multiple comparisons using either the Bonferroni approach or the false discovery rate (FDR).

Table 3.1 reports results from independent linear regression models (here without any adjustment for multiple comparisons) in selected exposures from our illustrative

Table 3.1: Single regressions for selected exposures in the simulated dataset

	Estimate	p.value
x3	0.078	0.007
x4	0.089	0.003
x5	0.068	0.005
x12	0.294	0.000
x13	0.238	0.000

example. These results seem to indicate that all exposures are independently associated with the outcome.

3.1.2 Multiple regression

Results from independent linear regression are hampered by the strong assumption that mixture components do not act as confounders of the association between each other component and the outcome of interest. This assumption is very seldom met in practice. A common situation, for example, is that two or more constituents of the mixture share one or more source, which usually results in moderate to high levels of correlation between exposures. Using DAGs, we can depict this situation as in Figure 3.2.

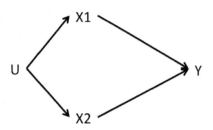

Figure 3.2: DAG for two exposures that share a common source

In this situation, a statistical model evaluating the association between X_1 and Y will need to adjust for X_2 to reduce the impact of bias due to residual confounding. In general, when any level of correlation exists between two mixture components, we do expect them to act as confounders of the association between the other exposure and the outcome. This implies that results from independent linear regressions are likely biased due to uncontrolled confounding. In our illustrative example, for instance, we know that X_{12} and X_{13} are highly correlated; results from independent linear regressions indicated that both exposures are positively associated with the outcome (Table 3.1), but these coefficients are probably biased. Mutually adjusting for the two exposures in the same statistical model is therefore required to account for such confounding and possibly identify whether both exposures are really associated with the outcome, or if the real driver of the association is just one of the two. Note that both situations are realistic: we might have settings where a specific exposure is biologically harmful (say X_{12}), and the association between the correlated one (X_{13}) and the outcome was a spurious result due to this high correlation, as well as settings where both exposures are really associated with the outcome (maybe because it is the source of exposure to have a direct effect). We need statistical methodologies that are able to detect and distinguish these possible scenarios.

The most intuitive way to account for co-confounding between mixture components is to mutually adjust for all exposures in the same regression model:

$$E[Y|X,C] = \beta_0 + \sum_{i=1}^{p} \beta_i \cdot X_i + \beta \cdot C$$

Table 3.2 presents results from a multiple regression that includes the 14 exposures in our example, as well as results from the chemical-specific models.

Table 3.2: Multiple and single regression results from the simulated dataset

	Estimate - multiple	p.value - multiple	Estimate - single	p.value - single
x1	0.058	0.080	0.106	0.001
x2	0.018	0.554	0.073	0.012
x3	-0.030	0.774	0.078	0.007
x4	0.053	0.044	0.089	0.003
x5	0.004	0.923	0.068	0.005
x6	0.060	0.047	0.120	0.000
x7	-0.031	0.620	0.153	0.000
x8	0.017	0.679	0.137	0.000
x9	0.025	0.673	0.160	0.000
x10	0.052	0.260	0.125	0.000
x11	0.049	0.341	0.149	0.000
x12	0.222	0.138	0.294	0.000
x13	-0.083	0.586	0.238	0.000
x14	0.054	0.293	0.185	0.000

3.1.3 The problem of multicollinearity

Results from the multiple regression are not consistent with those obtained from independent regression models, especially (and unsurprisingly) for those exposures that showed high levels of correlations. For example, within the exposure cluster $X_{12} - X_{13}$, the multiple regression model suggests that only X_{12} is associated with the outcome, while the coefficient of X_{13} is strongly reduced. Something similar happens for the $X_3-X_4-X_5$ cluster, where only X_4 remains associated with Y. Can we safely conclude that X_{12} and X_4 are associated with Y and that the other results were biased due to uncontrolled confounders? Before addressing this question, let's take a look at a published paper where we evaluated the performance of several statistical models to evaluate the association between a mixture of 8 phthalate metabolites and birth weight in a pregnancy cohort (Chiu et al. (2018)).[1] Figure 3.3 presents results from the 8 independent regressions and a multiple regression model. Figure 3.4 presents instead the correlation plot of the 8 metabolites.

---

[1] Content reproduced with permission from Elsevier

	β (one at the time)	p-value	β (mutually adjusted)	p-value
MiBP	-20.0	0.51	-6.8	0.84
MBzP	-24.7	0.34	-18.7	0.53
MEOHP	-23.7	0.33	247.1	0.11
MnBP	-28.5	0.31	-6.5	0.86
MEHHP	-28.2	0.24	-127.4	0.36
MECPP	-32.6	0.20	-82.8	0.32
MEP	-27.1	0.18	25.0	0.24
MEHP	-36.8	0.10	-59.0	0.18

Figure 3.3: Regression results from Chiu et al. 2018

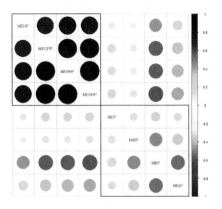

Figure 3.4: Correlation plot from Chiu et al. 2018

While we were expecting results from the two approaches to be different in the presence of high correlations, the coefficients obtained from the multiple regression leave room to a lot of skepticism. For example, the coefficients for MEOHP and MEHHP, when evaluated together, change respectively from -24 to 247, and from -28 to -127. Are these results reliable? Are we getting any improvement from to the biased results that we obtained from independent linear regressions?

The most common problem that arises when using multiple regression to investigate mixture-outcome association is multicollinearity (or simply collinearity). This occurs when independent variables in a regression model are correlated, with stronger consequences the higher the correlation. More specif-

44

ically, a high correlation between two predictors simultaneously included in a regression model will decrease the precision of their estimates and increase their standard errors. If the correlation between two covariates (say X_1 and X_2) is very high, then one is a pretty accurate linear predictor of the other. Collinearity does not influence the overall performance of the model, but has an important impact on individual predictors. In general (as a rule of thumb), given two predictors X_1 and X_2 that are associated with the outcome ($\beta = 0.2$ for both) when their correlation is equal to 0, the estimates in a linear model will be impacted by $\rho(X_1, X_2)$ as presented in Figure 3.5.

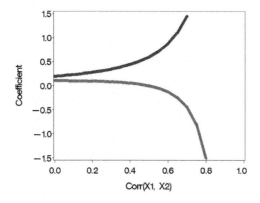

Figure 3.5: The reverse paradox

This issue, usually referred to as reverse paradox (the coefficients of 2 correlated covariates will inflate in opposite directions), is clearly affecting results from the paper presented above (the coefficients of highly correlated phthalate metabolites are either extremely large or extremely small), and possibly also results from the illustrative example (coefficients from correlated variables have opposite signs). Nevertheless, it should be noted that high correlation does not automatically imply that coefficients will be inflated. In another example (Bellavia et al. (2019)), for instance, we evaluated a mixture of three highly correlated parabens compounds, yet results from multiple regression were in line to those obtained

45

Table 3.3: VIFs from multiple regression results presented in Table 3.2

	x
x1	1.235658
x2	1.317951
x3	49.479946
x4	58.241935
x5	11.256382
x6	2.271043
x7	2.722583
x8	3.892965
x9	2.553431
x10	2.810535
x11	3.694404
x12	6.085748
x13	6.557098
x14	3.152092
z1	1.139690
z2	4.784064
z3	1.135437

from other mixture modeling techniques.

To quantify the severity of multicollinearity in a regression analysis one should calculate the Variance Inflation Factor (VIF). The VIF provides a measure of how much the variance of an estimated regression coefficient is increased because of collinearity. For example, if the VIF for a given predictors were 4, than the standard error of that predictors would be 2 times larger than if that predictor had 0 correlation with other variables. As a rule of thumb, VIFs above 4 should set the alarm off, as they indicate that those coefficients are likely affected by the high correlations between the corresponding predictor and other covariates in the model. Table 3.3 shows VIFs in our illustrative example, indicating that our results are deeply affected by multicollinearity. In this situation, alternative modeling options should be pursued.

3.2   Penalized regression approaches

An important set of models that can be very useful in the context of environmental mixtures are penalized regression approaches. These methods are directly built as extensions of standard OLS by incorporating a penalty in the loss function (hence the name). Their popularity in environmental epidemiology is due to the fact that this penalization procedure tends to decrease the influence of collinearity by targeting the overall variability of the model, thus improving the performance of the regression in the presence of high levels of correlations between included covariates. As always, however, everything comes for a price, and the improvement in the variance is achieved by introducing some bias (specifically, coefficients will be shrunk towards zero, reason why these approaches are also referred to as shrinkage procedures).

3.2.1   Bias-variance tradeoff

The word bias usually triggers epidemiologists' antennas, so it is important to understand what we mean by "introducing some bias" and how this can be beneficial in our context. To do so, let's begin by refreshing the basic math behind the estimation of a classical multiple regression. In linear regression modeling, we aim at predicting n observations of the response variable, Y, with a linear combination of m predictor variables, X, and a normally distributed error term with variance σ^2:

$$Y = X\beta + \epsilon$$
$$\epsilon \sim N(0, \sigma^2)$$

We need a rule to estimate the parameters, β, from the sample, and a standard choice to do so is by using ordinary least square (OLS), which produce estimates $\hat{\beta}$ by minimizing the sum of squares of residuals is as small as possible. In other words, we minimize the following loss function:

$$L_{OLS}(\hat{\beta}) = \sum_{i=1}^{n}(y_i - x_i'\hat{\beta})^2 = \|y - X\hat{\beta}\|^2$$

47

Using matrix notation, the estimate turns out to be :

$$\hat{\beta}_{OLS} = (X'X)^{-1}(X'Y)$$

To evaluate the performance of an estimator, there are two critical characteristics to be considered: its bias and its variance. The bias of an estimator measures the accuracy of the estimates:

$$Bias(\hat{\beta}_{OLS}) = E(\hat{\beta}_{OLS}) - \beta$$

The variance, on the other hand, measures the uncertainty of the estimates:

$$Var(\hat{\beta}_{OLS}) = \sigma^2(X'X)^{-1}$$

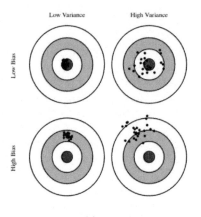

Source: kdnuggets.com

Figure 3.6: Archery example

Think of the estimator as an Olympic archer (Figure 3.6). The best performer will be an archer with low bias and low variance (top-left), who consistently aims the target for every estimate. An archer with low bias but high variance will be the one who will shoot inconsistently around the center (top-right), but we may also have an archer with high bias and low variance, who is extremely precise in consistently shooting at the wrong target (bottom-left). Now, the OLS estimator is an archer who is designed to be unbiased, but in certain situations might have a very high variance, situation that commonly happens when collinearity is a threat, as documented by the inflation in the variance calculated by the VIF.

To assess the overall performance of an estimator by taking into account both bias and variance, one can look at the Mean Squared Error (MSE), defined as the sum of Variance and squared Bias.

$$MSE = \frac{1}{n} \sum_{i=1}^{n} (Y_i - \hat{Y}_i)^2 = Var(\hat{\beta}) + Bias^2(\hat{\beta})$$

The basic idea of bias-variance trade-off is to introduce some bias in order to minimize the mean squared error in those situation where the performances of OLS are affected by high variance. This is achieved by augmenting the loss function through the introduction of a penalty. While there are several ways of achieving this, we will here focus on three common penalty functions that originate Ridge, LASSO, and Elastic-Net regression, with the latter being a generalized version of the previous two.

3.2.2 Ridge regression

Ridge regression augments the OLS loss function as to not only minimize the sum of squared residuals, but also penalize the size of the parameters estimates, shrinking them towards zero

$$L_{ridge}(\hat{\beta}) = \sum_{i=1}^{n} (y_i - x_i'\hat{\beta})^2 + \lambda \sum_{j=1}^{m} \hat{\beta}_j^2 = \|y - X\hat{\beta}\|^2 + \lambda \|\hat{\beta}\|^2$$

Minimizing this equation provides this solution for the parameters estimation:

$$\hat{\beta}_{ridge} = (X'X + \lambda I)^{-1}(X'Y)$$

where λ is the penalty and I an identity matrix.

We can notice that as $\lambda \to 0$, $\hat{\beta}_{ridge} \to \hat{\beta}_{OLS}$, while as $\lambda \to \infty$, $\hat{\beta}_{ridge} \to 0$. In words, setting λ to 0 is like using OLS, while the larger its value, the stronger the penalization. The unique feature of Ridge regression, as compared to other penalization techniques, is that coefficients can be shrunk over and over but will never reach 0. In other words, all covariates will always remain in the model, and Ridge does not provide any form of variable selection.

It can be shown that as λ becomes larger, the variance decreases and the bias increases. How much are we willing to trade? There are several approaches that can be used to choose for the best value of λ:

- Choose the λ that minimizes the MSE
- Use a traditional approach based on AIC or BIC criteria, to evaluate the performance of the model in fitting the data. While software tend to do the calculation automatically, it is important to remember that the degrees of freedom of a penalized model, needed to calculate such indexes, are different from the degrees of freedom of a OLS model with the same number of covariates/individuals
- Finally, a recommended procedure is based on cross-validation, focusing more on the predictive performances of the model. More specifically, to avoid the the model perfectly fits our data with poor generalizability (situation commonly known as overfitting in the machine learning vocabulary), we tend to select the model corresponding to the largest λ within one unit of standard deviation around the λ that minimizes the MSE

Let's turn to our illustrative example to see Ridge regression in practice. Given that both Ridge and LASSO are special cases of elastic net, we are going to use the `glmnet` package for all three approaches. Alternative approaches are available and could be considered. First we should define a set of potential values of λ that we will then evaluate (`lambdas_to_try`). To select the optimal λ we are then going to use the 10-fold cross validation approach, which can be conducted with the `cv.glmnet` command. Note that with option `standardize=TRUE` exposure will be standardized; this can be set to FALSE if standardization has been already conducted. Also, the option `alpha=0` has to be chosen to conduct Ridge regression (we will see later that Ridge is an Elastic Net model where an α parameter is equal to 0).

```
ridge_cv <- cv.glmnet(X, Y, alpha = 0,
                      lambda = lambdas_to_try,
                      standardize = TRUE,
                      nfolds = 1000)
```

We can now plot the MSE at different levels of λ. While the goal is to find the model that minimizes the MSE (`lambda.min`), we don't want the model to overfit our data. For this reason we tend to select the model corresponding to the largest λ within one unit of standard deviation around `lambda.min` (`lambda.1se`). Figure 3.7 shows the plot of MSE over levels of λ, also indicating these two values of interest (the vertical dashed lines).

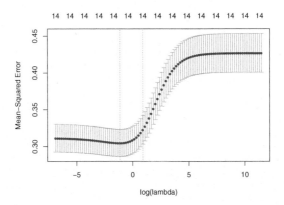

Figure 3.7: MSE vs lambda for Ridge regression in simulated data

```
# lowest lambda
lambda_cv_min <- ridge_cv$lambda.min
lambda_cv_min
```

[1] 0.3199267

```
# Best cross-validated lambda
lambda_cv <- ridge_cv$lambda.1se
lambda_cv
```

[1] 2.477076

Another useful figure is the trajectory of coefficients at varying levels of λ (Figure 3.8).

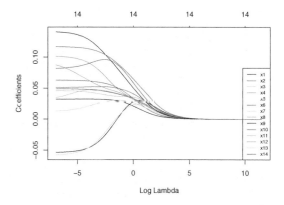

Figure 3.8: Coefficients trajectories for Ridge regression in simulated dataset

The starting values on the left of the figure are the ones from OLS estimation, and then we see how coefficients get shrunk at increasingly higher levels of λ. Note that the shrinkage is operated on the entire model, and for this reason individual trajectories are not necessarily forced to decrease (here some coefficients become larger before getting shrunk). Also, from the numbers plotted on top of the figure, indicating the number of coefficients that are still included in the model, we can see that coefficients only tend asymptotically to 0 but are never really removed from the model.

Finally, we can summarize the results of our final model for the selected value of lambda:

```
model_cv <- glmnet(X, Y, alpha = 0,
                   lambda = lambda_cv, standardize = TRUE)
```

These results, presented in Table 3.4, can provide some useful information but are of little use in our context. For example, we know from our VIF analysis that the coefficients for X_{12} and X_{13} are affected by high collinearity, but we would like to understand whether a real association exists for both exposures or whether one of the two is driving the cluster. To do so, we might prefer to operate some sort of variable selection,

53

Table 3.4: Ridge regression estimates in the simulated dataset

	Estimate
x1	0.013
x2	0.021
x3	0.024
x4	0.024
x5	0.020
x6	0.026
x7	0.029
x8	0.031
x9	0.030
x10	0.026
x11	0.024
x12	0.038
x13	0.031
x14	0.047

constructing a penalty so that non-influential covariates can be set to 0 (and therefore removed). This is what LASSO does.

3.2.3 LASSO

LASSO, standing for Least Absolute Shrinkage and Selection Operator, also adds a penalty to the loss function of OLS. However, instead of adding a penalty that penalizes sum of squared residuals (L2 penalty), LASSO penalizes the sum of their absolute values (L1 penalty). As a results, for high values of λ, many coefficients are exactly zeroed, which is never the case in Ridge regression (where 0s are the extreme case as $\lambda \to \infty$). Specifically, the LASSO estimator can be written as

$$L_{lasso}(\hat{\beta}) = \sum_{i=1}^{n}(y_i - x_i'\hat{\beta})^2 + \lambda \sum_{j=1}^{m}|\hat{\beta}_j|$$

As before, let's turn to our illustrative example to understand properties and interpretation. The procedure in R is exactly the same, with the only difference that the parameter α is set to 1. First, let's identify the optimal value of λ using the cross validation procedure (Figure 3.9),

```
lasso_cv <- cv.glmnet(X, Y, alpha = 1,
                      lambda = lambdas to_try,
                      standardize = TRUE,
                      nfolds = 1000)
```

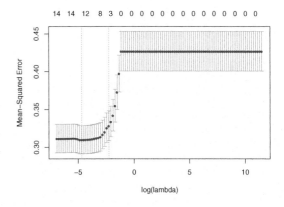

Figure 3.9: MSE vs lambda for LASSO regression in the simulated dataset

```
# lowest lambda
lambda_cv_min_lasso <- lasso_cv$lambda.min
lambda_cv_min_lasso
```

[1] 0.009326033

```
# Best cross-validated lambda
lambda_cv_lasso <- lasso_cv$lambda.1se
lambda_cv_lasso
```

[1] 0.1047616

and then plot the coefficients trajectories (Figure 3.10).

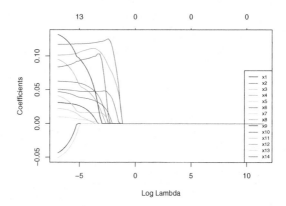

Figure 3.10: Coefficients trajectories for LASSO regression in the simulated dataset

We see that, differently from what observed in Ridge regression, coefficients are shrunk to a point where they exactly equal 0, and are therefore excluded from the model. The numbers on top of Figure 3.9 show how many exposures are left in the model at higher levels of λ. Finally, let's take a look at the results of the optimal selected model, presented in Table 3.5.

```
model_cv_lasso <- glmnet(X, Y, alpha = 1,
                         lambda = lambda_cv_lasso,
                         standardize = TRUE)
```

The final model selects only 4 covariates, while all others drop to 0. If we look at our two established groups of correlated exposures, X_4 and X_{12} are selected, while the others are left out.

In general, LASSO's results may be very sensitive to weak associations, dropping coefficients that are not actually 0. LASSO can set some coefficients to zero, thus performing variable selection, while Ridge regression cannot. The two methods solve multicollinearity differently: in Ridge

Table 3.5: LASSO regression estimatesin the simualated dataset

	Estimate
x1	0.000
x2	0.000
x3	0.000
x4	0.080
x5	0.000
x6	0.009
x7	0.000
x8	0.041
x9	0.000
x10	0.000
x11	0.000
x12	0.000
x13	0.000
x14	0.122

regression, the coefficients of correlated predictors are similar, while in LASSO, one of the correlated predictors has a larger coefficient, while the rest are (nearly) zeroed. LASSO tends to do well if there are a small number of significant parameters and the others are close to zero (that is - when only a few predictors actually influence the response). Ridge works well if there are many large parameters of about the same value (that is - when most predictors impact the response).

3.2.4 Elastic net

Rather than debating which model is better, we can directly use Elastic Net, which has been designed as a compromise between LASSO and Ridge, attempting to overcome their limitations and performing variable selection in a less rigid way than LASSO. Elastic Net combines the penalties of Ridge regression and LASSO, aiming at minimizing the following loss function

$$L_{enet}(\hat{\beta}) = \frac{\sum_{i=1}^{n}(y_i - x_i'\hat{\beta})^2}{2n} + \lambda \left(\frac{1-\alpha}{2} \sum_{j=1}^{m} \hat{\beta}_j^2 + \alpha \sum_{j=1}^{m} |\hat{\beta}_j| \right)$$

where α is the mixing parameter between Ridge ($\alpha=0$) and LASSO ($\alpha=1$). How this loss function is derived, given the Ridge and LASSO ones, is described in Zou and Hastie (2005). Procedures to simultaneously tune both α and λ to retrieve the optimal combinations are available and developed in the R package `caret`. For simplicity we will here stick on `glmnet`, which requires pre-defining a value for α. One can of course fit several models and compare them with common indexes such as AIC or BIC. To ensure some variable selection, we may for example choose a value of λ like 0.7, closer to LASSO than to Ridge. Let's fit an Elastic Net model, with $\alpha = 0.7$ in our example. First, we need to select the optimal value of λ (Figure 3.11).

```
enet_cv <- cv.glmnet(X, Y, alpha = 0.7,
                     lambda = lambdas_to_try,
                     standardize = TRUE,
                     nfolds = 1000)
```

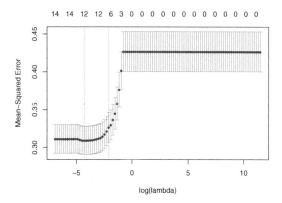

Figure 3.11: MSE vs lambda for elastic net regression in the simulated dataset

```
lambda_cv_min_enet <- enet_cv$lambda.min
lambda_cv_min_enet
```

[1] 0.01353048

```
# Best cross-validated lambda
lambda_cv_enet <- enet_cv$lambda.1se
lambda_cv_enet
```

[1] 0.1261857

and then plot the coefficients' trajectories (Figure 3.12).

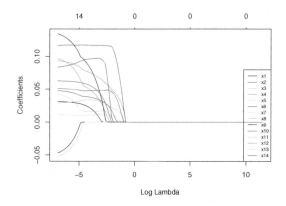

Figure 3.12: Coefficients trajectories for elastic net

We see that coefficients are shrunk to a point where they exactly equal 0, and therefore excluded from the model, but that this happens more conservatively as compared to LASSO (as documented from the numbers on top). Let's take a look at the results of the optimal selected model (Table 3.6).

```
model_cv_enet <- glmnet(X, Y, alpha = 0.7,
                        lambda = lambda_cv_enet,
                        standardize = TRUE)
```

As expected, less covariates are dropped to 0. Unfortunately, however, all components of the group of correlated covariates $X_3 - X_5$ remain in the model, and we are not able to identify the key actor of that group. Results, however, seem to agree with multiple regression in indicating X_6 and X_{12} as the main predictors of the outcome.

Penalized regression techniques allow including confounders, which can be done by specifying them in the model as in a regular OLS model. However, we may want them to be involved in the selection process. To such end, the best way is to include them in the matrix of covariates to be penalized, but inform the CV procedure that you don't want their coefficients

Table 3.6: Elstic Net regression estimates in the simulated dataset

	Estimate
x1	0.000
x2	0.000
x3	0.022
x4	0.050
x5	0.011
x6	0.018
x7	0.000
x8	0.046
x9	0.007
x10	0.000
x11	0.000
x12	0.009
x13	0.000
x14	0.116

to be modified. The following chunk of code will do that.

```
enet_cv_adj <- cv.glmnet(X, Y, alpha = 0.7,
            lambda = lambdas_to_try,
            standardize = TRUE, nfolds = 1000,
        penalty.factor=c(rep(1,ncol(X)-3),0,0,0))
```

3.2.5 Additional notes

Before moving to the next subsection, additional relevant details on penalized regression should be briefly discussed.

- Replicate results in classical OLS

When Elastic Net is used to describe associations in population-based studies, it is common practice to also present a final linear regression model that only includes those predictors that were selected from the penalized approach. This model will ensure better interpretation of the coefficients, and hopefully not be subject anymore to issues of collinearity that the selection should have addressed.

- Grouped LASSO

In some settings, the predictors belong to pre-defined groups, or we might have observed well-defined subgroups of exposures from our PCA. In this situation one may want to shrink and select together the members of a given group, which can be achieved with grouped LASSO. The next subsection will provide alternative regression approaches where preliminary grouping information can be used to address some limitations of standard regression.

- Time-to-event outcomes

Recent developments allow fitting Elastic Net with time-to-event outcomes, within the context of a regularized Cox regression model. Given the popularity of this method in epidemiology it is reasonable to expect that this approach will become more popular in the context of environmental mixture given that methods that were built ad-hoc do not always account for these types of outcomes. A first R package was develop in 2011 (`coxnet`)[2], and those algorithms for right-censored data have also been included in the most recent version of `glmnet`

- Non-linear associations

An implicit assumption we have made so far is that each covariate included in the model has a linear (or log-linear) effect

---

[2]https://cran.r-project.org/web/packages/glmnet/vignettes/Coxnet.pdf

on the outcome of interest. We know that this is often not true (several environmental exposures, for example, have some kind of plateau effect) and we might want to be able to incorporate non-linearities in our analyses. While classical regression can flexibly allow incorporating non-linearities by means of categorical transformations or restricted cubic splines, this is not of straightforward application in penalized regression. In complex settings where strong departures from linearity are observed in preliminary linear regressions, one should probably consider more flexible techniques such as BKMR (Section 5).

3.2.6 Elastic Net and environmental mixtures

Using Elastic Net to evaluate the association between a mixture of environmental exposures and a health outcome is becoming increasingly popular. A nice and rigorous application of the method can be found in Lenters et al. (2016), evaluating co-exposure to 16 chemicals as they relate to birth weight in 1250 infants.[3] Figure 3.13 presents the correlation plot from the manuscript.

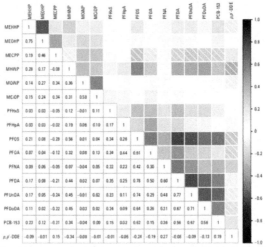

Figure 2 Spearman correlation coefficients between exposure biomarkers. The color intensity of shaded boxes indicates the magnitude of the correlation. Blue indicates a positive correlation, and red with white diagonal lines indicates a negative correlation.

Figure 3.13: Correlation plot from Lenters et al. 2016

Results presenting, respectively, the Elastic Net model, and the final OLS only including selected covariates, are presented in Figures 3.14 and 3.15.

---

[3]Figures and Tables here presented are reproduced from Environmental Health Perspectives with permission from the authors.

Table 2. Multiple-exposure elastic net penalized regression models[a] (β_{EN}) for term birth weight.

Potential predictor (increment)	Adjusted	Plus gestational age	Further adjusted
ln-MEHHP (1.70 ng/mL)	−64.67[b]	−59.43[b]	−48.61
ln-MEOHP (1.29 ng/mL)	−0.15	0	0
ln-MECPP (1.42 ng/mL)	0	0	0
ln-MHiNP (2.74 ng/mL)	0	0	0
ln-MOiNP (2.22 ng/mL)	23.81	22.26	16.31
ln-MCiOP (2.32 ng/mL)	0	0	0
ln-PFHxS (1.24 ng/mL)	−3.49	0	0
ln-PFHpA (1.84 ng/mL)	0	0	0
ln-PFOS (1.60 ng/mL)	0	0	0
ln-PFOA (1.18 ng/mL)	−11.51	−10.11	−38.82
ln-PFNA (1.03 ng/mL)	−7.05	−7.69	0
ln-PFDA (1.40 ng/mL)	0	0	0
ln-PFUnDA (2.10 ng/mL)	0	0	0
ln-PFDoDA (1.67 ng/mL)	−22.56	0	0
ln-PCB-153 (2.43 ng/g)	0	0	0
ln-p,p'-DDE (1.82 ng/g)	−106.39[b]	−76.63[b]	−47.02[b]

Regression coefficients (β_{EN}) represent the change in mean birth weight (g) for term infants per increment: a 2-SD increase in ln-transformed exposure biomarker levels. β_{EN} for the modeled, unpenalized covariates are not shown.
[a]The cross-validated optimum penalization was $\alpha = 1.00$, $\lambda = 3.32$ (MSE = 205,061) for the adjusted model (minimal sufficient set: study population, maternal age, prepregnancy BMI, and parity); $\alpha = 1.00$, $\lambda = 3.32$ (MSE = 177,179) for the model additionally adjusted for gestational age; and $\alpha = 0.98$, $\lambda = 2.46$ (MSE = 166,329) for the further adjusted model (plus infant sex, maternal height, alcohol consumption, serum cotinine, and vitamin D). All models, $n = 1,250$. [b]Covariance test

Figure 3.14: Elastic net regression results from Lenters et al. 2016

Table 3. Multiple-exposure unpenalized linear regression models for the exposures selected via elastic net regression and term birth weight [β_{OLS} (95% CI)].

Predictor (increment)	Adjusted	p-Value	Plus gestational age	p-Value	Further adjusted	p-Value
ln-MEHHP (1.70 ng/mL)	−86.75 (−139.18, −34.32)	0.001	−83.94 (−132.88, −35.19)	0.001	−70.22 (−117.59, −22.85)	0.004
ln-MOiNP (2.22 ng/mL)	45.85 (−4.84, 96.54)	0.076	45.62 (−1.51, 92.74)	0.058	37.64 (−7.99, 83.27)	0.106
ln-PFOA (1.18 ng/mL)	−42.77 (−108.19, 22.65)	0.200	−41.02 (−101.83, 19.80)	0.186	−63.77 (−122.83, −4.71)	0.035
ln-p,p'-DDE[a] (1.82 ng/g)	−134.73 (−191.93, −77.53)	< 0.001	−100.75 (−154.13, −47.36)	< 0.001	−66.70 (−119.38, −14.02)	0.013
Population						
Poland	−40.24 (−133.58, 53.11)	0.398	4.84 (−82.16, 91.85)	0.913	−93.16 (−183.72, −2.60)	0.044
Ukraine	−218.89 (−300.66, −137.13)	< 0.001	−142.98 (−219.73, −66.22)	< 0.001	−256.90 (−338.77, −175.02)	< 0.001
Maternal age (years)						
27–31	88.14 (23.05, 153.24)	0.008	80.01 (19.48, 140.53)	0.010	65.44 (6.74, 124.14)	0.029
32–45	30.53 (−42.52, 103.57)	0.413	38.08 (−29.83, 105.99)	0.272	37.19 (−28.83, 103.21)	0.270
BMI (8.62 kg/m²)	209.00 (155.53, 262.46)	< 0.001	191.37 (131.51, 231.22)	< 0.001	194.00 (145.42, 242.50)	< 0.001
Parity: multiparous	58.72 (−3.63, 121.06)	0.065	76.33 (18.32, 134.34)	0.010	85.92 (29.39, 142.44)	0.003
Gestational age (2.45 weeks)			343.78 (295.61, 391.94)	< 0.001	330.43 (283.70, 377.15)	< 0.001
Infant sex: female					−115.40 (−160.36, −70.43)	< 0.001
Maternal height (12.93 cm)					135.83 (88.38, 183.28)	< 0.001
Alcohol: ≥ 7 drinks/week					34.43 (−61.76, 130.62)	0.483
Cotinine (113.51 ng/mL)					−140.41 (−191.92, −88.89)	< 0.001
Vitamin D (22.05 ng/mL)					18.77 (−29.39, 66.93)	0.445

Regression coefficients (β_{OLS}) represent the change in mean birth weight (g) for term infants per increment: a 2-SD increase in ln-transformed exposure biomarker or untransformed continuous covariate levels, or per category for categorical covariates. Reference categories are population, Greenland; maternal age, 18–26 years; nulliparous; infant sex, male; alcohol, < 7 drinks/week (around the time of conception). Variance inflation factors for exposure terms ranged from 1.04 to 1.74.
[a]β_{OLS} for models including wet weight p,p'-DDE (ng/mL), adjusted for total lipids: −134.22 (95% CI: −191.43, −77.02), −99.91 (95% CI: −153.30, −46.52), −67.16 (95% CI: −119.80, −14.51).

Figure 3.15: Final results from Lenters et al. 2016

Another application that thoroughly reports methods presentation, stating all assumptions and clearly discussing the results, can be found in Vriens et al. (2017), evaluating environmental pollutants and placental mitochondrial DNA content in infants.

3.3 Additional regression-based approaches

Before moving on to the a general discussion on advantages and limitations of regression-based approaches, and introduce and motivate further methods for environmental mixtures, it is useful to provide a broad overview of some alternative approaches based on, or derived from, classical regression that have proven useful in this context.

3.3.1 Hierarchical linear models

Hierarchical modeling allows improving performances of a multiple regression model when clustering of exposures can be clearly identified. Application of this approach for multiple exposures was first introduced to evaluate the effect of antiretroviral treatments in HIV epidemiology, where several drugs belonging to clearly defined drug classes are usually defined (Correia and Williams (2019)). In brief, the model incorporates first-stage effects for each drug class, and second-stage effects for individual drugs, assuming that the effect of each drug is the summation of the (fixed) effect of its drug class and a residual effect specific to the individual drug. Assuming that we can identify (or observe from preliminary analysis such as a PCA) well characterized subgroups of environmental exposures, this modeling technique can be used to improve the performance of multiple regression when focusing on environmental mixtures. Potential advantages include the absence of variable selection and shrinkage, thus allowing a better interpretation of results.

3.3.2 Partial least square regression

The Partial least square (PLS) regression can be seen as a method that generalizes and combines PCA and multiple regression. PLS regression is very useful to predict dependent variables from a very large number of predictors that might be highly correlated. The PLS regression replaces the initial independent variable space (X) and the initial response variable space (Y) by smaller spaces that rely on a reduced number of variables named latent variables, which are included one by one in an iterative process. The sparse PLS (sPLS) regression, in particular, is an extension of PLS that aims at combining variable selection and modeling in a one-step procedure (Lê Cao et al. (2008)). Components are defined iteratively such that they explain as much as possible of the remaining covariance between the predictors and the outcome. The sPLS approach simultaneously yields good predictive performance and appropriate variable selection by creating sparse linear combinations of the original predictors. Sparsity is induced by including a penalty in the estimation of the linear combination coefficients, that is, all coefficients with an absolute value lower than some fraction of the maximum absolute coefficient are shrunk to zero. Only the first K components are included as covariates in a linear regression model. sPLS is available in the R package `spls`.[4] A detailed illustration of using sPLS in environmental epidemiology can be found in Lenters et al. (2015).

3.4 Advantages and limitations of regression approaches

Together with underlying some of the limitations of single and multiple regression in evaluating the effects of environmental mixtures on health outcomes, primarily due to the main problem of multicollinearity, this section has also introduced techniques that overcome such limitation while remaining embedded in a regression framework. Among these techniques, review articles and simulation studies agree in concluding that penalized regression consistently outperformed conventional approaches, and that the choice of what method to use should be selected based on one-by-one situation. A systematic comparison of methods based on regression in exposome-health analyses, also including additional techniques, can be found in Agier et al. (2016).

In practical settings, several research questions can be addressed by using multiple regression or its extensions. Nevertheless, there might be research questions that are beyond

---

[4]https://cran.r-project.org/web/packages/spls/vignettes/spls-example.pdf

the reach of regression techniques and for which some additional methodologies should be considered.

- Assessing the overall mixture effect.

Penalized approaches addressed the issues of collinearity and high-dimension by operating some sort of variable selection. While this allows retrieving information on the actual effects for each selected component, addressing other questions such as the ones related to the overall effect of the mixture can not be evaluated. As discussed in Section 1, this is a relevant research question that is often of primary interest in environmental epidemiology. The next section will address this problem, introducing the weighted quantile sum (WQS) regression framework as a technique to evaluate the overall effect of an environmental mixture while taking into account high levels of correlation.

- Complex scenarios with several exposures and interactive mechanisms.

When the mixture of interest is composed by several exposures, it is likely that the mixture-outcome association will involve non-linear and interactive mechanisms. As the number of potential predictors gets higher, so does the complexity of the model. In such situations the performances of regression-based approaches are generally weak, and more flexible algorithms should be taken into considerations. These problems will be assessed in section 5, introducing Bayesian Kernel Machine Regression as a flexible non-parametric approach to estimate the mixture-outcome association in the presence of complex non-linear and interactive mechanisms, and then discussing techniques for the assessment of high-dimensional interactions, including machine learning algorithms based on trees modeling.

Chapter 4

Assessing the overall effect of multiple exposures

Extensions of linear regression presented in the previous chapter address the complexity of the mixture-outcome association by selecting relevant predictors within the mixture, thus removing covariates that would create problems due to high collinearity, or simply by reducing the dimension of the exposure matrix thus improving the fit of the model. This approach, however, also comes with relevant drawbacks.

Let's think of the group of highly correlated exposures from our hypothetical example $(X_3 - X_4 - X_5)$, where penalized approaches recommended only selecting X_4. This allowed evaluating the independent effect of X_4 on the outcome without being troubled by the high levels of correlation between this covariate and the other two of the cluster. This same selection, however, is preventing us to address other important questions. For example, what if there is an interaction between X_3 and X_4 (this can happen even if X_3 does not have an independent effect on the outcome, but only an effect that is triggered in the presence of the other co-exposure)? By removing X_3 from the model, we will not be able to evaluate this interaction. Moreover, we will not be able to correctly quantify the joint effect of X_3 and X_4, which is the sum of the two main effects and their 2-way interaction. As discussed in the first chapter, this is a very important research question; the three correlated exposures might for instance come from the same source, and quantifying their joint effect would in this case provide useful information on the public health benefits of reducing exposure to the source.

The question that we will address in this section is the following: how do we quantify the joint effect of several exposures, possibly highly correlated, when regression techniques are not functional?

4.1 Unsupervised summary scores

A very intuitive approach to address this question is to create one or more summary score(s) that summarize individual levels of exposure to the mixture, thus reducing the number of covariates that are going to be evaluated. A very common example of such approach is used by investigators working on phthalates. In this context, analyses are often hampered by the presence of extreme correlation between metabolites of Di(2-ethylhexyl)phthalate (DEHP), and researchers are commonly summarizing this information into a molar sum of DEHP metabolites. Li et al. (2019) writes, for example "we calculated the molar sum of DEHP metabolites (ΣDEHP) by dividing each metabolite concentration by its molecular weight and then summing: ΣDEHP=[MEHP (g/L)$\times$(1/278.34 (g/mol))]+[MEHHP (g/L) $\times$ (1/294.34 (g/mol))] + [MEOHP (g/L) $\times$ (1/292.33 (g/ mol))] + [MECPP (g/L) $\times$ (1/308.33 (g/mol))]." Note that, with this approach, the score targets a selected sub-sample of exposures (the highly-correlated cluster creating problems), and other phthalates metabolites are included in the model without any transformation.

Another common approach is to use components derived from PCA, as described in section 2. PCA allows identifying continuous covariates that summarize the variability of the mixture exposure. Including these derived components into a regression model has the great advantage that all collinearity issues will be resolved, as the components are uncorrelated by definition. On the other hand, the validity of this approach is severely affected by whether the obtained components have clear biological interpretation. An example of application of this approach in environmental epidemiology can be found in Souter et al. (2020).

4.2 The Weighted Quantile Sum (WQS) and its extensions

Taking one step further, researchers might be interested in taking into account the relationship between the exposures and the outcome while summarizing the complex exposure to the mixture of interest. The weighted quantile sum (WQS), developed specifically for the context of environmental mixtures analysis, is an increasingly common approach that allows evaluating a mixture-outcome association by creating a summary score of the mixture in a supervised fashion (Czarnota, Gennings, and Wheeler (2015)), (Carrico et al. (2015)). Specifically, WQS is a statistical model for multivariate regression in high-dimensional dataset that operates in a supervised framework, creating a single score (the weighted quantile sum) that summarizes the overall exposure to the mixture, and by including this score in a regression model to evaluate the overall effect of the mixture on the outcome of interest. The score is calculated as a weighted sum (so that exposures with weaker effects on the outcome have lower weight in the index) of all exposures categorized into quartiles, or more groups, so that extreme values have less impact on the weights estimation.

4.2.1 Model definition and estimation

A WQS regression model takes the following form:

$$g(\mu) = \beta_0 + \beta_1 \left(\sum_{i=1}^{c} w_i q_i \right) + z'\varphi$$

The $\sum_{i=1}^{c} w_i q_i$ term represents the index that weights and sums the components included in the mixture. As such, β_1 will be the parameter summarizing the overall effect to the (weighted) mixture. In addition, the model will also provide an estimate of the individual weights w_i that indicate the relative importance of each exposure in the mixture-outcome association.

To estimate the model, the data may be split in a training and a validation dataset: the first one to be used for the weights estimation, the second one to test for the significance of the final WQS index. The weights are estimated through a bootstrap and constrained to sum to 1 and to be bounded between 0 and 1: $\sum_{i=1}^{c} w_i = 1$ and $0 \leq w_i \leq 1$. For each bootstrap sample (usually $B = 100$ total samples) a dataset is created sampling with replacement from the training dataset and the parameters of the model are estimated through an optimization algorithm.

Once the weights are estimated, the model is fitted in order to find the regression coefficients in each ensemble step. After the bootstrap ensemble is completed, the estimated weights are averaged across bootstrap samples to obtain the WQS index:

$$WQS = \sum_{i=1}^{c} \bar{w}_i q_i$$

Typically weights are estimated in a training set then used to construct a WQS index in a validation set, which can be used to test for the association between the mixture and the health outcome in a standard generalized linear model, as:

$$g(\mu) = \beta_0 + \beta_1 WQS + z^{'}\varphi$$

After the final model is complete one can test the significance of the β_1 to see if there is an association between the WQS index and the outcome. In the case the coefficient is significantly different from 0 then we can interpret the weights: the highest values identify the associated components as the relevant contributors in the association. A selection threshold can be decided a priori to identify those chemicals that have a significant weight in the index.

4.2.2 The unidirectionality assumption

WQS makes an important assumption of uni-direction (either a positive or a negative) of all exposures with respect to the outcome. The model is inherently one-directional, in that it tests only for mixture effects positively or negatively associated with a given outcome. In practice, analyses should therefore be run twice to test for associations in either direction.

The one-directional index allows not to incur in the reversal paradox when we have highly correlated variables thus improving the identification of bad actors.

4.2.3 Extensions of the original WQS regression

- Dependent variables

The WQS regression can be generalized and applied to multiple types of dependent variables. In particular, WQS regression has been adapted to four different cases: logistic, multinomial, Poisson and negative binomial regression. For these last two cases it is also possible to fit zero-inflated models keeping the same objective function used to estimate the weights as for the Poisson and negative binomial regression but taking into account the zero inflation fitting the final model.

- Random selection

A novel implementation of WQS regression for high-dimensional mixtures with highly correlated components was proposed in Curtin et al. (2021). This approach applies a random selection of a subset of the variables included in the mixture instead of the bootstrapping for parameter estimation. Through this method we are able to generate a more de-correlated subsets of variables and reduce the variance of the parameter estimates compared to a single analysis. This extension was shown to be more effective compared to WQS in modeling contexts with large predictor sets, complex correlation structures, or where the numbers of predictors exceeds the number of subjects.

- Repeated holdout validation for WQS regression

One limit of WQS is the reduced statistical power caused by

the necessity to split the dataset in training and validation sets. This partition can also lead to unrepresentative sets of data and unstable parameter estimates. A recent work from Tanner, Bornehag, and Gennings (2019) showed that conducing a WQS on the full dataset without splitting in training and validation produces optimistic results and proposed to apply a repeated holdout validation combining cross-validation and bootstrap resampling. They suggested to repeatedly split the data 100 times with replacement and fit a WQS regression on each partitioned dataset. Through this procedure we obtain an approximately normal distribution of the weights and the regression parameters and we can apply the mean or the median to estimate the final parameters. A limit of this approach is the higher computational intensity.

- Other extensions

To complete the set of currently available extensions of this approach, it is finally worthy to mention the Bayesian WQS (Colicino et al. (2020)), which also allows relaxing the uni-directional assumption, and the lagged WQS (Gennings et al. (2020)), which deals with time-varying mixtures of exposures to understand the role of exposure timing.

4.2.4   Quantile G-computation

A recent paper by Keil et al. (2020) introduced an additional modeling technique for environmental mixture that builds up on WQS regression integrating its estimation procedure with g-computation. This approach, called Quantile-based g-Computation estimates the overall mixture effect with the same procedure used by WQS, but estimating the parameters of a marginal structural model, rather than a standard regression. In this way, under common assumptions in causal inference such as exchangeability, causal consistency, positivity, no interference, and correct model specification, this model will also improve the causal interpretation of the overall effect. Importantly, the procedure also allegedly overcomes the assumption of uni-direction, and the flexibility of marginal structural models also allows incorporating non-linearities in the contribution of each exposure to the score. Additional details on the models can be found on the original paper or in the very useful R introductory vignette available online.[1]

4.2.5 WQS regression in R

WQS is available in the R package gWQS (standing for generalized WQS).[2] The recently developed quantile G-computation approach is instead available in the qgcomp package.

Fitting WQS in R will require some additional data management as both gWQS and qgcomp will require an object with the names of the exposures, rather than a matrix with the exposures themselves.

```
exposure<- names(data2[,3:16])
```

The following lines will fit a WQS regression model for the positive direction, with a 40-60 training validation split, and without adjusting for covariates. The reader can refer to the online vignette for details on all available options.

```
results1 <- gwqs(y ~ wqs, mix_name = exposure,
            data = data2, q = 4, validation = 0.6,
            b = 10, b1_pos = T, b1_constr = F,
            family = "gaussian", seed = 123)
```

After fitting the model, this line will produce a barplot with the weights as well as the summary of results (overall effect and weights estimation), presented in Table 4.1 and Figure 4.1.

```
gwqs_barplot(results1, tau=NULL)
```

---

[1]https://cran.r-project.org/web/packages/qgcomp/vignettes/qgcomp-vignette.html

[2]https://cran.r-project.org/web/packages/gWQS/vignettes/gwqs-vignette.html

Table 4.1: WQS: weights estimation in the simulated dataset

	mix_name	mean_weight
x12	x12	0.2080444
x5	x5	0.1990505
x4	x4	0.1860921
x6	x6	0.1190146
x8	x8	0.1120772
x2	x2	0.0586329
x1	x1	0.0518465
x9	x9	0.0295788
x14	x14	0.0224343
x7	x7	0.0074698
x13	x13	0.0057590
x3	x3	0.0000000
x10	x10	0.0000000
x11	x11	0.0000000

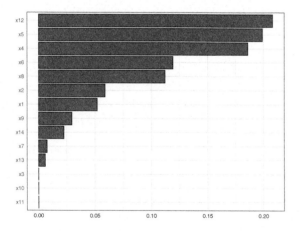

Figure 4.1: WQS: weights estimation in the simulated dataset

To estimate the negative index, still without direct constraint on the actual β, we change the b1_pos option to FALSE. In our example, all bootstrap samples provide a positive coefficient. This suggests that we are in a situation where all covariates have a positive (or null) effect. Even constraining the coefficient would likely not make any difference in this case - coefficients would either be all around 0, or the model will not converge.

To adjust the positive WQS regression model for confounders we can add them in the model as presented here:

```
results1_adj<-gwqs(y ~ wqs+z1+z2+z3,
                   mix_name = exposure, data = data2,
                   q = 4, validation = 0.6, b = 10,
                   b1_pos = T, b1_constr = F,
                   family = "gaussian", seed = 123)

gwqs_barplot(results1_adj, tau=NULL)
```

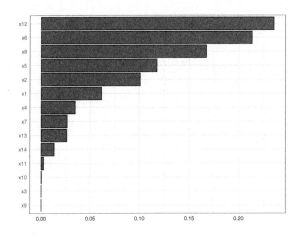

Figure 4.2: WQS: weights estimation with covariates adjustment in the simulated dataset

After adjustment the association is largely attenuated, and the weights of the most important contributors change both in magnitude as well as in ranking (Figure 4.2). This implies that the three confounders have a different effect on each of the components (e.g. the contribution of X_6 was attenuated before adjusting, while the contribution of X_4 was overestimated).

The following lines will instead fit a quantile G-computation model. What we have to specify in the command is the list of exposures, the name of the mixture object, the data, the type of outcome (continuous here), and whether we want quartiles or other categorizations. Weights estimates are presented in Figure 4.3.

```
qc <- qgcomp(y ~ x1+x2+x3+x4+x5+x6+x7+x8+x9+x10+
               x11+x12+x13+x14+z1+z2+z3,
               expnms=exposure, data2,
               family=gaussian(), q=4)

plot(qc)
```

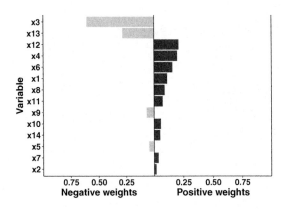

Figure 4.3: qgcomp: weights estimation with covariates adjustment in the simulated dataset

The Authors also recommended fitting the model using bootstrap, which can be achieved with the following command. Note that the number of iterations, here set to 10, should be at least 200. The plot from this model will provide the estimate of the overall effect of the mixture (Figure 4.4).

```
qc.boot <- qgcomp.boot(y ~ x1+x2+x3+x4+x5+x6+x7+
                           x8+x9+x10+x11+x12+x13
                           +x14+z1+z2+z3,
                           expnms=exposure, data2,
                           family=gaussian(), q=4,
                           B=10, seed=123)

plot(qc.boot)
```

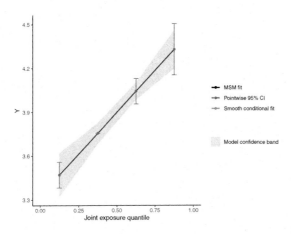

Figure 4.4: qgcomp: overall mixture effect in the simulated dataset

It is interesting to note that in this situation of high-collinearity, qgcomp's results are still affected as we see a strikingly high (and, as we know since data are simulated, wrong) negative weight for X_3.

As a final note please consider that both packages are very recent and constantly updated and revised. One should always refer to online vignettes and documentations for updates and eventual modification in the syntax.

4.2.6 Example from the literature

Thanks for its easy implementation in statistical software and the development of the several discussed extensions, WQS is

79

rapidly becoming one of the most common techniques used by investigators to evaluate environmental mixtures.

As an illustrative example on how methods and results can be presented the reader can refer to a paper from Deyssenroth et al. (2018), evaluating the association between 16 trace metals, measured in post-partum maternal toe nails in about 200 pregnant women from the Rhode Island Child Health Study, and small for gestational age (SGA) status. Before fitting WQS the Authors conduct a preliminary analysis using conditional logistic regression, which indicates that effects seem to operate in both directions. As a consequence, WQS results are presented for both the positive and negative directions, summarizing both weights estimates and total effects in a clear and informative figure.

Chapter 5

Flexible approaches for complex settings

In the previous sections we have discussed the challenges that arise when evaluating environmental mixtures and the several available techniques based on regression modeling that can be used to address different research questions in this context. The final part of section 3 discussed the two major limitations shared by all regression techniques, namely the difficulties in estimating overall mixture effects and to include additional model complexities such as non-linearities and (possibly high-order) interactions. In the previous section we have discussed WQS as a useful tool to address the first limitation. Note than, interestingly, this technique can be actually seen as yet another regression extension, as it is based on integrating a summary score into a generalized linear model.

To tackle the second challenge, let's first note that any regression would allow integrating interactions of any order (this is done by simply including product terms between any pair, or higher combination, of exposures) as well as non-linear associations. Splines modeling is probably the best way of accounting for non-linear effects in regression modeling, or one can also consider using generalized additive models (GAM), which have been successfully applied in the context of environmental mixtures (Zheng et al. (2020)). Nevertheless, both the inclusion of product terms and spline transformations will rapidly increase the number of parameters that have to be estimated, and we might be in need of alternative techniques that can more flexibly tackle these issues. We are going to describe two approaches: first, Bayesian Kernel Machine Regression (BKMR), a method specifically developed for evaluating environmental mixtures that is increasing in popularity because of its several advantages and flexibility (Bobb et al. (2015),Bobb et al. (2018)). Second, the use of machine learning techniques, and specifically tree-based modeling such as boosted regression trees (Lampa et al. (2014),Bellavia et al. (2021)). Additional techniques that can be considered when the specific focus is on detecting interactions will not be discussed here, and the reader can refer to these publications summarizing and discussing methodologies in this context: Barrera-Gómez et al. (2017), Sun et al. (2013).

5.1 Bayesian Kernel Machine Regression

5.1.1 Introduction

Bayesian Kernel Machine Regression (BKMR) is designed to address, in a flexible non-parametric way, several objectives such as detection and estimation of an effect of the overall mixture, identification of pollutant or group of pollutants responsible for observed mixture effects, visualizing the exposure-response function, or detection of interactions among individual pollutants. The main idea of BKMR is to model exposure through means of a kernel function. Specifically, the general modeling framework is:

$$Y_i = h(z_{i1}, ..., z_{iM}) + \beta x_i + \epsilon_i$$

where Y_i is a continuous, normally distributed health endpoint, h is a flexible function of the predictor variables $z_{i1}, ..., z_{iM}$, and x_i is a vector of covariates assumed to have a linear relationship with the outcome

There are several choices for the kernel function used to represent h. The focus here is on the Gaussian kernel, which flexibly captures a wide range of underlying functional forms for h and can accommodate nonlinear and non-additive effects of the multivariate exposure. Specifically, the Gaussian kernel implies the following representation for h:

$$K_{vs}(z_i, z_j) = exp\{-\sum_M r_m(z_{im} - z_{jm})^2\}$$

Intuitively, the kernel function shrinks the estimated health effects of two individuals with similar exposure profiles toward each other. The weights r_m present the probability that each exposure is important in the function, with $r_m = 0$ indicating that there is no association between the mth exposure and the outcome. By allowing some weights to be 0, the method is implicitly embedding a variable selection procedure. This can also integrate information on existing structures among exposures (e.g. correlation clusters, PCA results, similar mechanisms ...) with the so-called hierarchical variable selection, which estimates the probability that each group of exposures is important, and the probability that, given a group is important, each exposure in that group is driving that group-outcome association.

5.1.2   Estimation

BKMR takes its full name from the Bayesian approach used for estimating the parameters. The advantages of this include the ability of estimating the importance of each variable (r_m) simultaneously, estimating uncertainties measures, and easily extending the estimation to longitudinal data. Since the estimation is built within an iterative procedure (MCMC), variable importance are provided in terms of Posterior Inclusion Probability (PIP), the proportion of iterations with $r_m > 0$. Typically, several thousands of iterations are required.

The `bkmr` R package developed by the authors makes implementation of this technique relatively straightforward.[1] Using our illustrative example, the following chunk of code presents a set of lines that are required before estimating a BKMR model. Specifically, we are defining the object containing the

---

[1] https://jenfb.github.io/bkmr/overview.html

mixture $(X_1 - X_{14})$, the outcome (Y), and the confounders $(Z_1 - Z_3)$. We also need to generate a seed (we are using an iterative process with a random component) and a knots matrix that will help speeding up the process. This final step is very important as the model estimation can be extremely long (the recommendation is to use a number of knots of more or less n/10).

```
mixture<-as.matrix(data2[,3:16])
y<-data2$y
covariates<-as.matrix(data2[,17:19])

set.seed(10)
knots100  <- fields::cover.design(mixture,
                                  nd = 50)$design
```

The actual estimation of a BKMR model is very simple and requires one line of R code. With the following code we fit a BKMR model with Gaussian predictive process using 100 knots. We are using 1000 MCMC iterations for the sake of time, but a final analysis should be run on a much larger number of samples, up to 50000. Here we are allowing for variable selection, but not providing any information on grouping.

```
temp <-  kmbayes(y=y, Z=mixture, X=covariates,
                 iter=1000, verbose=FALSE,
                 varsel=TRUE, knots=knots100)
```

The ExtractPIPs() command will show one of the most important results, the posterior inclusion probabilities, shown in Table 5.1. We can interpret this output as the variable selection part, in which we get information on the importance of each covariate in defining the exposures-outcome association. In descending order, the most important contribution seems to come from $X_{12}, X_6, X_{10}, X_2, X_{14}, X_{11}$. This is in agreement with Elastic Net and WQS, which also identified X_{12} and X_6 as the most important contributors. Also note that within the other cluster we haven't yet been able to understand who the bad actor is, if any exists.

Table 5.1: Posterior Inclusion Probabilities in the simulated dataset

variable	PIP
x1	0.110
x2	0.082
x3	0.000
x4	0.000
x5	0.072
x6	0.142
x7	0.000
x8	0.336
x9	0.062
x10	0.400
x11	0.188
x12	0.818
x13	0.080
x14	0.158

5.1.3 Trace plots and burning phase

Since we are using several iterations it is important to evaluate the convergence of the parameters. These can be checked by looking at trace plots (what we expect here is some kind of random behavior around a straight line). What we generally observe is an initial phase of burning, which we should remove from the analysis. Here, we are removing the first 100 iterations and this number should be modify depending on the results of your first plots (Figures 5.1 and 5.2).

```
sel<-seq(0,1000,by=1)

TracePlot(fit = temp, par = "beta", sel=sel)
```

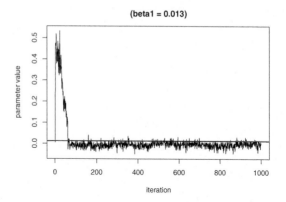

Figure 5.1: Convergence plot for a single parameter without exclusions

```
sel<-seq(100,1000,by=1)

TracePlot(fit = temp, par = "beta", sel=sel)
```

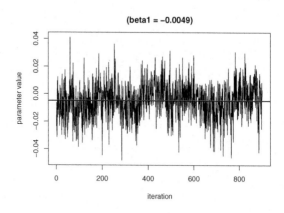

Figure 5.2: Convergence plot for a single parameter after burning phase exclusion

5.1.4 Visualizing results

After estimation of a BKMR model, which is relatively straightforward and just requires patience throughout iterations, most of the work will consist of presenting post-estimation figures that can describe the complex relationship between the mixture and the outcome. The R package includes several functions to summarize the model output in different ways and to visually display the results.

To visualize the exposure-response functions we need to create different dataframes with the predictions that will be then graphically displayed with ggpolot.

```
pred.resp.uni <- PredictorResponseUnivar(fit=temp,
                                         sel=sel,
                                    method="approx")

pred.resp.bi  <- PredictorResponseBivar(fit=temp,
                              min.plot.dist = 1,
                        sel=sel,  method="approx")

pred.resp.bi2 <- PredictorResponseBivarLevels(
                 pred.resp.df = pred.resp.bivar,
                 Z = mixture, both_pairs=TRUE,
                      qs = c(0.25, 0.5, 0.75))

risks.overall <- OverallRiskSummaries(fit=temp,
                       qs=seq(0.25, 0.75, by=0.05),
                                   q.fixed = 0.5,
                      method = "approx", sel=sel)

risks.singvar <- SingVarRiskSummaries(fit=temp,
                       qs.diff = c(0.25, 0.75),
                    q.fixed = c(0.25, 0.50, 0.75),
                          method = "approx")

risks.int <- SingVarIntSummaries(fit=temp,
                      qs.diff = c(0.25, 0.75),
                     qs.fixed = c(0.25, 0.75))
```

The first three objects will allow us to examine the predictor-response functions, while the next three objects will calculate a range of summary statistics that highlight specific features of the surface.

5.1.4.1 Univariate dose-responses

One cross section of interest is the univariate relationship between each covariate and the outcome, where all of the other exposures are fixed to a particular percentile (Figure 5.3). This can be done using the function PredictorResponseUnivar. The argument specifying the quantile at which to fix the other exposures is given by q.fixed (the default value is q.fixed = 0.5).

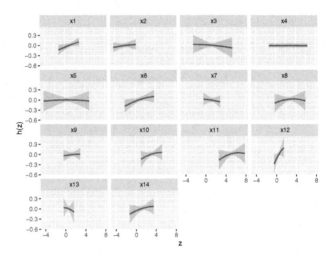

Figure 5.3: Univariate dose-response associations from BKMR in the simulated dataset

These figures seem to indicate that all selected covariates have weak to moderate associations with the outcome, and that all dose-responses seem to behave in a linear fashion.

5.1.4.2 Bivariable exposure-response functions

This is the plot of the `PredictorResponseBivar` function, which visualizes the bivariate exposure-response function for two predictors, where all of the other predictors are fixed at a particular percentile (Figure 5.4).

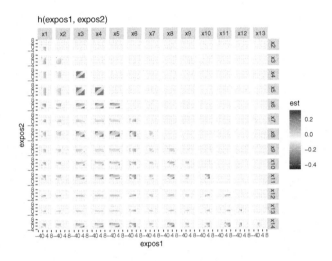

Figure 5.4: Bivariate exposure-response associations from BKMR in the simulated dataset

5.1.4.3 Interactions

Figure 5.4 might not be the most intuitive way of checking for interactions. An alternative approach is to investigate the predictor-response function of a single predictor in Z for a given second predictor in Z fixed at various quantiles (and for the remaining predictors fixed to a specific value). These plots can be obtained using the `PredictorResponseBivarLevels` function, which takes as input the bivariate exposure-response function outputted from the previous command, where the argument `qs` specifies a sequence of quantiles at which to fix the second predictor. From the full set of combinations (Figure 5.5) we can easily select a specific one that we want to present, like the $X_6 - X_{12}$ one (Figure 5.6).

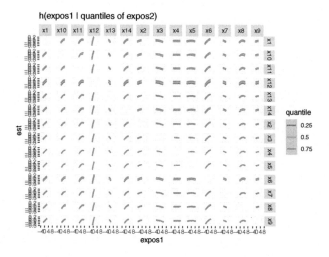

Figure 5.5: Qualitative interaction assessment from BKMR in the simulated dataset

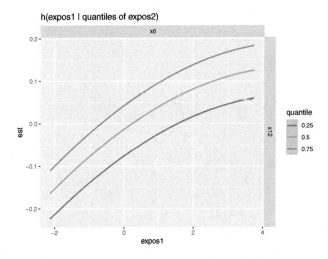

Figure 5.6: Qualitative interaction assessment between X6 and x12 from BKMR in the simulated dataset

These figures do not provide any evidence of interactions throughout the mixture. As we know, this is correct since no interactions were specified in the simulated dataset.

5.1.4.4 Overall mixture effect

Another interesting summary plot is the overall effect of the mixture (function OverallRiskSumamries), calculated by comparing the value of h when all predictors are set to a particular percentile as compared to when all of them are set to their 50th percentile (Figure 5.7).

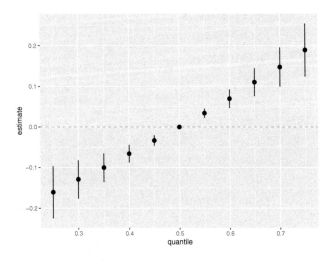

Figure 5.7: Overall Mixture Effect from BKMR in the simulated dataset

In agreement with WQS, higher exposure to the overall mixture is associated with higher expected value of the outcome.

5.1.4.5 Single variables effects

This additional function (`SingVarRiskSumamries`) summarizes the contribution of an individual predictor to the response. For example, we may wish to compare the outcome when a single predictor in h is at the 75th percentile as compared to when that predictor is at its 25th percentile, setting all of the remaining predictors at a specific percentile (Figure 5.8).

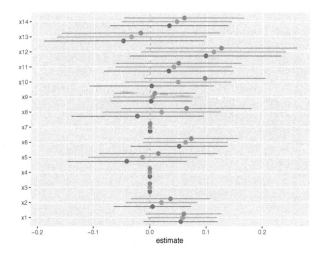

Figure 5.8: Individual effects from BKMR in the simulated dataset

5.1.4.6 Single variable interaction terms

Finally, this function (`SingVarIntSumamries`) is similar to the latest one, but refers to the interaction of a single exposure with all other covariates. It attempts to represent an overall interaction between that exposure and all other components (Figure 5.9).

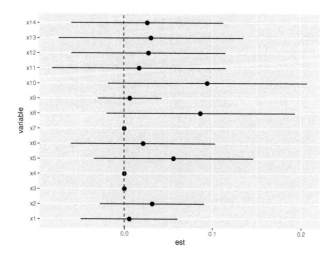

Figure 5.9: Individual interaction effects from BKMR in the simulated dataset

As observed before, this graph also leads us to conclude that we have no evidence of interaction for any covariate.

5.1.5 Hierarchical selection

The variable selection procedure embedded into BKMR can also operate within a hierarchical procedure. Using our example, we could for instance inform the model that there are highly correlated clusters of exposures. This will allow us to get an estimate of the relative importance of each cluster and of each exposure within it. The procedure is implemented as follows, where we are specifically informing the model that there is a cluster of three highly correlated covariates:

```
hier <- kmbayes(y=y, Z=mixture, X=covariates,
        iter=1000, verbose=FALSE, varsel=TRUE,
        knots=knots100,
        groups=c(1,1,2,2,2,1,1,1,1,1,1,1,1,1))
```

Group PIPs, shown in Table 5.2, seem to point out that the cluster is somehow relevant in the dose-response association,

Table 5.2: Posterior Inclusion Probabilities from Hierarchical BKMR in the simulated dataset

variable	group	groupPIP	condPIP
x1	1	1.000	0.0000000
x2	1	1.000	0.0000000
x3	2	0.044	0.3636364
x4	2	0.044	0.4545455
x5	2	0.044	0.1818182
x6	1	1.000	0.0160000
x7	1	1.000	0.0040000
x8	1	1.000	0.0620000
x9	1	1.000	0.0540000
x10	1	1.000	0.0000000
x11	1	1.000	0.0020000
x12	1	1.000	0.4500000
x13	1	1.000	0.1460000
x14	1	1.000	0.2660000

and indicates that that X_4 might be the most relevant of the three exposures.

5.1.6 BKMR Extensions

The first release of BKMR was only available for evaluating continuous outcomes, but recent work has extended its use to the context of binary outcomes, which are also integrated in the latest versions of the package. Domingo-Relloso et al. (2019) have also described how to apply BKMR with time-to-event outcomes. Additional extensions of the approach that could be of interest in several settings also include a longitudinal version of BKMR based on lagged regression, which can be used to evaluate time-varying mixtures (Liu et al. (2018)). While this method is not yet implemented in the package, it is important to note that similar results can be achieved by evaluating time-varying effects through hierarchical selection. In brief, multiple measurements of exposures can be included simultaneously in the kernel, grouping exposures by time. An example of this application can be found in Tyagi et al. (2021), evaluating exposures to phthalates during pregnancy, measured at different trimester, as they relate to final gestational weight. By providing a measure of group importance, group PIPs can here be interpreted as measures of relative importance of the time-windows of interest, thus allowing a better understanding of the timing of higher susceptibility to mixture exposures.

5.1.7 Practical considerations and discussion

To conclude our presentation of BKMR, let's list some useful considerations that one should take into account when applying this methodology:

- As a Bayesian technique, prior information could be specified on the model parameters. Nevertheless this is not commonly done, and all code presented here is assuming the use of non-informative priors. In general, it is good to remember that PIP values can be sensitive to priors (although relative importance tends to be stable).
- Because of their sensitivity, PIP values can only be interpreted as a relative measure of importance (as ranking the importance of exposures). Several applied papers have been using thresholds (e.g. 0.5) to define a variable as "important," but this interpretation is erroneous and misleading.
- The BKMR algorithm is more stable when it isn't dealing with exposures on vastly different scales. We typically center and scale both the outcome and the exposures (and continuous confounders). Similarly, we should be wary of exposure outliers, and log-transforming exposures is also recommended.
- BKMR is operating a variable selection procedure. As such, a PIP of 0 will imply that the dose-response for that covariate is a straight line on zero. This does not mean that a given exposure has no effect on the outcome, but simply that it was not selected in the procedure. As a matter of fact, when an exposure has a weak effect on the outcome BKMR will tend to exclude it. As a consequence of this, the overall mixture effect will really present the overall effect of the selected exposures.

- As a Bayesian technique, BKMR is not based on the classical statistical framework on null-hypothesis testing. 95% CIs are interpreted as credible intervals, and common discussions on statistical power should be avoided.
- Despite the estimation improvements through the use of knots as previously described, fitting a BKMR model remains time-demanding. In practice, you might be able to fit a BKMR model on a dataset of up to 10.000 individuals (still waiting few hours to get your results). For any larger dataset, alternative approaches should be considered.
- BKMR is a flexible non-parametric method that is designed to deal with complex settings with non-linearities and interactions. In standard situations, regression methods could provide a better estimation and an easier interpretation of results. In practical terms, you would never begin your analysis by fitting a BKMR model but only get to it for results validation or if alternative techniques were not sufficiently equipped to deal with your data.

5.2 Assessing interactions

5.2.1 Tree-based modeling

In settings where one is interested in formally evaluating interactions, unique challenges are involved. First, we already discussed how evaluating several covariates and high-order interactions within a regression framework will rapidly increase the number of parameters to be estimated, and the resulting complexity of the model will make classical regression techniques of little use. Summary and classification approaches like WQS will not be able to provide an estimate of interaction effects, and we have just discussed how BKMR can only provide some qualitative assessment of interactions, and only among those exposures that have passed the selection procedure.

To account for the complexity of joint effects and high-dimensional interactions, one should consider techniques that have been specifically develop to deal with complex and big data. One machine learning (ML) approach that can be useful in the context of interaction analysis, and specifically when evaluating environmental exposures, is the application of boosted regression trees (BRT). BRT is a tree-based modeling technique that can be used to evaluate complex high-dimensional interactions among several variables, which can be continuous, categorical, or binary. Boosted trees are designed to improve the performance of classification and regression trees (CARTs), which partition the data into several disjoint regions approximating the outcome as constant within these regions. CARTs can account for complex interactions by conditioning subsequent splits on previous ones, a feature that is controlled by a "depth" option. Higher-order depths correspond to accounting for higher-order interactions. In practical terms, this implies that by modifying the depth option of the algorithm we can incorporate an increasingly higher number of interaction orders. How many interactions should be evaluated, together with other parameters of the model, are identified by the machine through cross validation techniques.

Boosted trees improve the predictive performance of a single

CART by combining several weak learners to accurately identify a set of explanatory variables that are associated with the outcome. The improved predictive performance, however, will come at the expense of an easy interpretation. Specifically, the output of a BRT will provide identification of variable importance, partial dependence plot, and interactions hierarchy, but will not provide effect estimates for each variable or interaction as in classical regression. A BRT model will provide the following objects as output:

- Variable importance: this is based on how many times each variable is involved in a split, capturing its independent predictive power with respect to the outcome. This measure holds similar interpretation of PIPs in BKMR

- Dependence plots: similarly to the univariate dose-responses in BKMR, these provide a graphical visualization of the fitted function that presents the associations between one or more predictors and the outcome. These plots are especially helpful with continuous predictors, but let's stress that this technique can be used with any kind of exposures.

- H-statistics: these are the unique measures of interaction relevance, which indicate, for any pair of predictors, the fraction of variance that is not captured by the sum of the two fitted response functions. Of importance, depending on the depth of the algorithm, H-statistics can be calculated for all levels of interactions including 2-way and more. These measures do not provide a summary of relative importance (i.e. they do not sum up to 1) but rather indicate a ranking of importance of interactions.

For more details on boosted trees we refer to previous publications (Lampa et al. (2014)) and online documentation.[2]

5.2.2 Interaction screening and regression approaches

Both BKMR, which provide a qualitative graphical assessment of interactions, and BRT models, which allow estimat-

---

[2]http://uc-r.github.io/gbm_regression

ing H-statistics to rank interactions of different orders, do not provide direct estimates or tests for interactions effects. For this reason, a recommended practice is to use these techniques as interaction screening procedures and employ a 2-steps approach in which selected interactions are then evaluated in a final regression model. As an illustrative example, the reader can refer to a recent publication where we used this approach to identify 2-ways interactions between occupational exposures and health factors that we later integrated in a regression models evaluating the effect of this mixture on ALS risk (Bellavia et al. (2021)).[3]

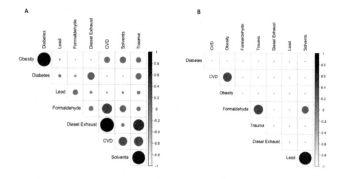

Figure 5.10: H-statistics from Bellavia et al. 2021

---

[3]Figure reproduced with permission from Elsevier

Chapter 6

Additional topics and final remarks

The aim of this last section is to provide a very brief introduction to additional topics that are often of relevance when investigating the health effects of multiple environmental exposures. First, we will provide a general overview of the extent to which what has been discussed so far can be evaluated from a causal inference perspective. Next, we will describe some relatively common situations where additional methodological considerations are required, namely the presence of zero-inflated or binary exposures. Finally, we will present an introductory overview of approaches that allow incorporating multiple exposures in mediation analysis, which is often a primary goal of exposome research.

6.1 Causal mixture effects

To improve our understanding of the associations between environmental exposures and health outcomes, and facilitate the development of more stringent public health regulations and interventions, it is important to determine the extent to which these associations reflect causal relationships. To establish causal links, researchers are advocating the use of a pluralistic approach in terms of study design, to reduce the potential harm due to typical epidemiological bias such as confounding or selection bias, as well in terms of statistical methodologies for causal inference (Vandenbroucke, Broadbent, and Pearce (2016), Dominici and Zigler (2017)). In the specific case of environmental exposures, this switch from association to causation has to account for the co-occurrence of multiple components or constituents, present in the real world as a complex mixture. At this time, regulatory policies are still mostly designed to regulate one pollutant or chemical at the time, thus hampering the implementation of integrated policies and possibly resulting in uncertainties about the exact impact of regulations. For this reason, several researchers, as well as and both governmental and private institutions, are increasingly advocating for more research that could improve our understanding of the causal effects of environmental mixtures accounting for the complex exposure to high-dimensional data.

The first step to improve findings interpretation towards a causal perspective is to focus on study design and pre-analytic considerations. The paper from Dominici and Zigler (2017) provides an excellent introduction that tackles these issues in the context of air pollution epidemiology, but can easily be extended to any set of environmental exposures. Another important contribution in terms of pre-analytic aspects was provided by Weisskopf and Webster (Weisskopf, Seals, and Webster (2018), Webster and Weisskopf (2020)) who have discussed the issue of bias amplification when evaluating environmental mixtures. Their work directly addresses issues of co-confounding related bias, presenting direct acyclic graphs (DAGs) in different contexts of interest.

After these pre-analytic aspects have been taken into consideration, the focus can be transferred to the statistical approaches that can be used to improve the causal understanding of mixture-outcome associations. Here several points should be mentioned:

- As the exposures mixture gets more and more complex, the time spent on the pre-processing phase (unsupervised analysis) will be more and more important.

- After this pre-processing phase, the assessment of the

mixture-outcome effect should be conducted in two stages. First, by using some of the techniques described here (WQS, BKMR, tree-based methods ...) one can identify a set of exposures (and interactions) that can be included in a causal model that will later be investigated in a secondary step.

- This 2-stages approach is highly recommended because most of the available methodologies for causal inference are based on extensions of regression techniques (e.g. propensity score, difference in differences, marginal structural models, inverse probability weighting). If the setting is not too complex (i.e. those settings where multiple regression is a potentially good choice), one can directly build the regression-based causal inference technique. A good introduction of causal inference techniques based on regression that can be useful in environmental epidemiology was provided by Bind (2019).

- Out of the possible methods for causal inference, a versatile option in the context of environmental mixtures is the multivariate version of the generalized propensity score (mvGPS), which we have applied and described in the context of air pollution epidemiology in a recent publication (Traini et al. (2021)).

- Finally, it is useful to remember that one of the recent extensions of WQS (quantile G-comp) was developed with the aim of improving the causal interpretation of the estimated weights and overall effect and could be used to provide a validation of the cumulative mixture effect from a causal perspective.

6.2 Binary and zero-inflated exposures

The common setting that we have described so far was making the implicit assumption that we are dealing with a set of multiple continuous exposures (e.g. concentrations of chemicals or pollutants) of joint interest. One important caveat, however, is that continuous exposures evaluated in this context are usually highly skewed (they are strictly non-negative). Log-transformation are commonly used, but these are ineffective when several values are zero. Zero-inflated exposures are skewed covariates with a lot of zeros, typically occurring in environmental epidemiology when several individuals have values below the limit of detection. Removing those individuals from the study (that is, considering the information as missing) might reduce power and, most importantly, does not reflect real levels of exposures (it would silence all effects occurring at low levels of exposures). Common alternative options include dicothomization of each exposure into detected/non detected, the use of categorical exposures, or imputation of non-detected values. Even with the latter, however, in the presence of a high number of zeros we would end up getting inflated covariates with a large proportion of individuals with the same exposure value (in practical terms, we might find it hard to really consider the exposure as continuous). If one wants to include zero-inflated covariates in the mixture without any transformation, available techniques include zero inflated poisson models (ZIP), zero-inflated negative binomial models (ZINB), or hurdle models.

When exposures are instead dicothomized (or, in general, when the interest is to evaluate multiple binary exposures), some additional techniques can be considered:

- First of all, evaluating the crude association between binary exposures, as we presented earlier with the correlation matrix, can be done using the ϕ coefficients, with $\phi = \chi^2/n$.
- Correspondence analysis: This will graphically display all covariates based on their proximity. We can think of this approach as an unsupervised method to investigate and depict patterns of exposures

- Hierarchical models and penalized methods can be used with binary exposures. If all covariates are binary, you may prefer not to standardize in order to improve interpretation.
- For high dimensional data, extensions of the regression and classification tree approaches for binary data have been developed, both unsupervised and supervised (e.g. CART/MARS, logic regression). BRT can be used with binary exposures.

6.3 Integrating environmental mixtures in mediation analysis

Mediation analysis is a common approach to investigate causal pathways relating the exposure(s) and the outcome of interest. When evaluating environmental mixtures, there are several settings where our mixture of interest is only a component of an even larger picture. For example, we may want to integrate sources of exposures, or evaluate the contribution of environmental chemicals to health disparities. Our mixture, in these cases, is a mediator of a given $X - Y$ association. In other settings, we might be interested in the mechanisms through which the mixture affects the outcome. The mixture here is the exposure in a mediation model. We can also have several mixtures affecting each other, or potential causal dependencies within the mixture itself.

In the general framework of exposome analysis, the underlying hypothesis is that a set of multiple exogenous exposures (the external exposome) affects the complex set of biomarkers at the microbiome level (the internal exposome), thus contributing to the development of health effects. The DAG in Figure 6.1, on the other hand, presents a common situation where researchers might be interested in evaluating an integrative framework for environmental exposures (E), lifestyle and behavioral factors (B), and social constructs (X), which may be complex but has the potential to elucidate mechanisms through which diseases are caused. This framework was presented in an introductory publication by Bellavia et al. (2018).

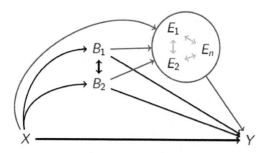

Figure 6.1: Integrated framework for environmental health disparities

Integrating methods for environmental exposures into mediation analysis has been the goal of several recent papers, which the reader could refer to for further details (Bellavia, James-Todd, and Williams (2019)), (Blum et al. (2020)), (Devick et al. (2018)). These methods have been largely unexplored in applied studies and may represent a critical tool to further identify the mechanisms through which the exposome affects human health. A recent R function was also developed to integrate BKMR into a mediation analysis context (Wang et al. (2020)).

6.4 Final remarks

The goal of this introductory course (and book) was to discuss the challenges involved in the study of environmental mixtures as they relate to health outcomes, and introduce the most common statistical approaches that can help addressing some of these challenges. The core points of the discussion were the following:

- Environmental mixtures represent the way environmental exposures occur and operate in real life and, as such, should be integrated and evaluated in environmental epidemiology studies. This involves a series of analytic and statistical issues that should be carefully addressed and taken into account.

- A first critical classification of statistical methodologies is the one between supervised and unsupervised approaches. It is always recommended to begin the analyses with a thorough pre-processing phase that involves unsupervised techniques. These will help identifying clustering and groupings of exposures, high levels of correlations, missingness, and the presence of inflated covariates, crucially guiding subsequent steps.

- When incorporating the outcome into the picture (supervised approaches) it it always recommended to begin with regression-based approaches. These provide unique advantages and most of the times will provide a good fit to the question of interest.

- Specific methods have been developed to address environmental mixtures when regression techniques are of little use or more flexible approaches are required. This occurs, for example, when high-dimensional interactions are of interests, if most associations are non-linear, or if the primary interest is in retrieving the cumulative mixture effect. Generally, all techniques come with some limitations and it is always recommended to test several methods and validate results providing different perspectives.

- With a very large number of exposures and/or interactions, machine learning (ML) techniques should be considered. Recent extensions of random forests such as gradient boosting machines (or boosted regression trees) provide several advantages in this context. Proceeding with different layers of analysis, using ML results to build a second-step regression model, is recommended.

- Most current methods are available and well documented/presented in the statistical software R.

- In general, when dealing with environmental exposures, the choice of the methods should be drive by the research question of interest.

  - Are there repeated exposures patterns? (unsupervised analysis, e.g. PCA)
  - What are the effects of individual exposures within the mixture? (regression methods, BKMR)
  - What are the most important contributors to the association? (PIPs in BKMR, weights from WQS, selected covariates in elastic net ...)
  - What is the overall (cumulative) effect of the mixture? (regression methods, WQS)
  - Are there interactions (or even synergies) between chemicals? (tree-based modeling, BKMR, regression methods)

Several papers have discussed different techniques and can provide further guidance to choose the correct approach. Recommended reading in this context include Hamra and Buckley (2018), Stafoggia et al. (2017), and Gibson et al. (2019).

As a final note, it is useful to remind that the material here presented is just a selection of topics out of a wide and fast-growing research area. Methodological extensions and new applications are continuously published and it is crucial for researchers working in this area to keep up with the literature.

References

Agier, Lydiane, Lützen Portengen, Marc Chadeau-Hyam, Xavier Basagaña, Lise Giorgis-Allemand, Valérie Siroux, Oliver Robinson, et al. 2016. "A Systematic Comparison of Linear Regression–Based Statistical Methods to Assess Exposome-Health Associations." *Environmental Health Perspectives* 124 (12): 1848–56.

Barrera-Gómez, Jose, Lydiane Agier, Lützen Portengen, Marc Chadeau-Hyam, Lise Giorgis-Allemand, Valérie Siroux, Oliver Robinson, et al. 2017. "A Systematic Comparison of Statistical Methods to Detect Interactions in Exposome-Health Associations." *Environmental Health* 16 (1): 1–13.

Bellavia, Andrea, Yu-Han Chiu, Florence M Brown, Lidia Mínguez-Alarcón, Jennifer B Ford, Myra Keller, John Petrozza, et al. 2019. "Urinary Concentrations of Parabens Mixture and Pregnancy Glucose Levels Among Women from a Fertility Clinic." *Environmental Research* 168: 389–96.

Bellavia, Andrea, Aisha S Dickerson, Ran S Rotem, Johnni Hansen, Ole Gredal, and Marc G Weisskopf. 2021. "Joint and Interactive Effects Between Health Comorbidities and Environmental Exposures in Predicting Amyotrophic Lateral Sclerosis." *International Journal of Hygiene and Environmental Health* 231: 113655.

Bellavia, Andrea, Tamarra James-Todd, and Paige L Williams. 2019. "Approaches for Incorporating Environ-

mental Mixtures as Mediators in Mediation Analysis."
Environment International 123: 368–74.

Bellavia, Andrea, Ami R Zota, Linda Valeri, and Tamarra
James-Todd. 2018. "Multiple Mediators Approach
to Study Environmental Chemicals as Determinants
of Health Disparities." *Environmental Epidemiology
(Philadelphia, Pa.)* 2 (2).

Bind, Marie-Abèle. 2019. "Causal Modeling in Environmental Health." *Annual Review of Public Health* 40: 23–43.

Blum, Michaël GB, Linda Valeri, Olivier François, Solène Ca-
diou, Valérie Siroux, Johanna Lepeule, and Rémy Slama.
2020. "Challenges Raised by Mediation Analysis in a High-
Dimension Setting." *Environmental Health Perspectives*
128 (5): 055001.

Bobb, Jennifer F, Birgit Claus Henn, Linda Valeri, and
Brent A Coull. 2018. "Statistical Software for Analyzing
the Health Effects of Multiple Concurrent Exposures via
Bayesian Kernel Machine Regression." *Environmental
Health* 17 (1): 1–10.

Bobb, Jennifer F, Linda Valeri, Birgit Claus Henn, David C
Christiani, Robert O Wright, Maitreyi Mazumdar, John
J Godleski, and Brent A Coull. 2015. "Bayesian Kernel
Machine Regression for Estimating the Health Effects of
Multi-Pollutant Mixtures." *Biostatistics* 16 (3): 493–508.

Carrico, Caroline, Chris Gennings, David C Wheeler, and
Pam Factor-Litvak. 2015. "Characterization of Weighted
Quantile Sum Regression for Highly Correlated Data in a
Risk Analysis Setting." *Journal of Agricultural, Biological,
and Environmental Statistics* 20 (1): 100–120.

Chiu, Yu-Han, Andrea Bellavia, Tamarra James-Todd,
Katharine F Correia, Linda Valeri, Carmen Messerlian,
Jennifer B Ford, et al. 2018. "Evaluating Effects of
Prenatal Exposure to Phthalate Mixtures on Birth
Weight: A Comparison of Three Statistical Approaches."
Environment International 113: 231–39.

Colicino, Elena, Nicolo Foppa Pedretti, Stefanie A Busgang,

and Chris Gennings. 2020. "Per-and Poly-Fluoroalkyl Substances and Bone Mineral Density: Results from the Bayesian Weighted Quantile Sum Regression." *Environmental Epidemiology (Philadelphia, Pa.)* 4 (3).

Correia, Katharine, and Paige L Williams. 2019. "A Hierarchical Modeling Approach for Assessing the Safety of Exposure to Complex Antiretroviral Drug Regimens During Pregnancy." *Statistical Methods in Medical Research* 28 (2): 599–612.

Curtin, Paul, Joshua Kellogg, Nadja Cech, and Chris Gennings. 2021. "A Random Subset Implementation of Weighted Quantile Sum (WQSRS) Regression for Analysis of High-Dimensional Mixtures." *Communications in Statistics-Simulation and Computation* 50 (4): 1119–34.

Czarnota, Jenna, Chris Gennings, and David C Wheeler. 2015. "Assessment of Weighted Quantile Sum Regression for Modeling Chemical Mixtures and Cancer Risk." *Cancer Informatics* 14: CIN–S17295.

Devick, Katrina L, Jennifer F Bobb, Maitreyi Mazumdar, Birgit Claus Henn, David C Bellinger, David C Christiani, Robert O Wright, Paige L Williams, Brent A Coull, and Linda Valeri. 2018. "Bayesian Kernel Machine Regression-Causal Mediation Analysis." *arXiv Preprint arXiv:1811.10453.*

Deyssenroth, Maya A, Chris Gennings, Shelley H Liu, Shouneng Peng, Ke Hao, Luca Lambertini, Brian P Jackson, Margaret R Karagas, Carmen J Marsit, and Jia Chen. 2018. "Intrauterine Multi-Metal Exposure Is Associated with Reduced Fetal Growth Through Modulation of the Placental Gene Network." *Environment International* 120: 373–81.

Domingo-Relloso, Arce, Maria Grau-Perez, Laisa Briongos-Figuero, Jose L Gomez-Ariza, Tamara Garcia-Barrera, Antonio Dueñas-Laita, Jennifer F Bobb, et al. 2019. "The Association of Urine Metals and Metal Mixtures with Cardiovascular Incidence in an Adult Population from Spain: The Hortega Follow-up Study." *International Journal of*

Epidemiology 48 (6): 1839–49.

Dominici, Francesca, Roger D Peng, Christopher D Barr, and Michelle L Bell. 2010. "Protecting Human Health from Air Pollution: Shifting from a Single-Pollutant to a Multi-Pollutant Approach." *Epidemiology (Cambridge, Mass.)* 21 (2): 187.

Dominici, Francesca, and Corwin Zigler. 2017. "Best Practices for Gauging Evidence of Causality in Air Pollution Epidemiology." *American Journal of Epidemiology* 186 (12): 1303–9.

Gennings, Chris, Paul Curtin, Ghalib Bello, Robert Wright, Manish Arora, and Christine Austin. 2020. "Lagged WQS Regression for Mixtures with Many Components." *Environmental Research* 186: 109529.

Gibson, Elizabeth A, Yanelli Nunez, Ahlam Abuawad, Ami R Zota, Stefano Renzetti, Katrina L Devick, Chris Gennings, Jeff Goldsmith, Brent A Coull, and Marianthi-Anna Kioumourtzoglou. 2019. "An Overview of Methods to Address Distinct Research Questions on Environmental Mixtures: An Application to Persistent Organic Pollutants and Leukocyte Telomere Length." *Environmental Health* 18 (1): 1–16.

Hamra, Ghassan B, and Jessie P Buckley. 2018. "Environmental Exposure Mixtures: Questions and Methods to Address Them." *Current Epidemiology Reports* 5 (2): 160–65.

Hevey, David. 2018. "Network Analysis: A Brief Overview and Tutorial." *Health Psychology and Behavioral Medicine* 6 (1): 301–28.

Keil, Alexander P, Jessie P Buckley, Katie M O'Brien, Kelly K Ferguson, Shanshan Zhao, and Alexandra J White. 2020. "A Quantile-Based g-Computation Approach to Addressing the Effects of Exposure Mixtures." *Environmental Health Perspectives* 128 (4): 047004.

Lampa, Erik, Lars Lind, P Monica Lind, and Anna Bornefalk-Hermansson. 2014. "The Identification of Complex Interactions in Epidemiology and Toxicology: A Simulation

Study of Boosted Regression Trees." *Environmental Health* 13 (1): 1–17.

Langfelder, Peter, and Steve Horvath. 2008. "WGCNA: An r Package for Weighted Correlation Network Analysis." *BMC Bioinformatics* 9 (1): 1–13.

Lee, Wan-Chen, Mandy Fisher, Karelyn Davis, Tye E Arbuckle, and Sanjoy K Sinha. 2017. "Identification of Chemical Mixtures to Which Canadian Pregnant Women Are Exposed: The MIREC Study." *Environment International* 99: 321–30.

Lenters, Virissa, Lützen Portengen, Anna Rignell-Hydbom, Bo AG Jönsson, Christian H Lindh, Aldert H Piersma, Gunnar Toft, et al. 2016. "Prenatal Phthalate, Perfluoroalkyl Acid, and Organochlorine Exposures and Term Birth Weight in Three Birth Cohorts: Multi-Pollutant Models Based on Elastic Net Regression." *Environmental Health Perspectives* 124 (3): 365–72.

Lenters, Virissa, Lützen Portengen, Lidwien AM Smit, Bo AG Jönsson, Aleksander Giwercman, Lars Rylander, Christian H Lindh, et al. 2015. "Phthalates, Perfluoroalkyl Acids, Metals and Organochlorines and Reproductive Function: A Multipollutant Assessment in Greenlandic, Polish and Ukrainian Men." *Occupational and Environmental Medicine* 72 (6): 385–93.

Lê Cao, Kim-Anh, Debra Rossouw, Christele Robert-Granié, and Philippe Besse. 2008. "A Sparse PLS for Variable Selection When Integrating Omics Data." *Statistical Applications in Genetics and Molecular Biology* 7 (1).

Li, Ming-Chieh, Lidia Mínguez-Alarcón, Andrea Bellavia, Paige L Williams, Tamarra James-Todd, Russ Hauser, Jorge E Chavarro, and Yu-Han Chiu. 2019. "Serum Beta-Carotene Modifies the Association Between Phthalate Mixtures and Insulin Resistance: The National Health and Nutrition Examination Survey 2003–2006." *Environmental Research* 178: 108729.

Liu, Shelley H, Jennifer F Bobb, Kyu Ha Lee, Chris Gennings, Birgit Claus Henn, David Bellinger, Christine Austin, et al.

2018. "Lagged Kernel Machine Regression for Identifying Time Windows of Susceptibility to Exposures of Complex Mixtures." *Biostatistics* 19 (3): 325–41.

Sanchez, Tiffany R, Vesna Slavkovich, Nancy LoIacono, Alexander van Geen, Tyler Ellis, Steven N Chillrud, Olgica Balac, et al. 2018. "Urinary Metals and Metal Mixtures in Bangladesh: Exploring Environmental Sources in the Health Effects of Arsenic Longitudinal Study (HEALS)." *Environment International* 121: 852–60.

Souter, Irene, Andrea Bellavia, Paige L Williams, TIM Korevaar, John D Meeker, Joseph M Braun, Ralph A de Poortere, et al. 2020. "Urinary Concentrations of Phthalate Metabolite Mixtures in Relation to Serum Biomarkers of Thyroid Function and Autoimmunity Among Women from a Fertility Center." *Environmental Health Perspectives* 128 (6): 067007.

Stafoggia, Massimo, Susanne Breitner, Regina Hampel, and Xavier Basagaña. 2017. "Statistical Approaches to Address Multi-Pollutant Mixtures and Multiple Exposures: The State of the Science." *Current Environmental Health Reports* 4 (4): 481–90.

Sun, Zhichao, Yebin Tao, Shi Li, Kelly K Ferguson, John D Meeker, Sung Kyun Park, Stuart A Batterman, and Bhramar Mukherjee. 2013. "Statistical Strategies for Constructing Health Risk Models with Multiple Pollutants and Their Interactions: Possible Choices and Comparisons." *Environmental Health* 12 (1): 1–19.

Tanner, Eva M, Carl-Gustaf Bornehag, and Chris Gennings. 2019. "Repeated Holdout Validation for Weighted Quantile Sum Regression." *MethodsX* 6: 2855–60.

Taylor, Kyla W, Bonnie R Joubert, Joe M Braun, Caroline Dilworth, Chris Gennings, Russ Hauser, Jerry J Heindel, Cynthia V Rider, Thomas F Webster, and Danielle J Carlin. 2016. "Statistical Approaches for Assessing Health Effects of Environmental Chemical Mixtures in Epidemiology: Lessons from an Innovative Workshop." *Environmental Health Perspectives* 124 (12): A227–29.

Traini, Eugenio, Anke Huss, Lützen Portengen, Matti Rookus, WM Monique Verschuren, Roel Vermeulen, and Andrea Bellavia. 2021. "A Multi-Pollutant Approach to Estimate the Causal Effects of Air Pollution Mixtures on Overall Mortality in a Large Prospective Cohort of Dutch Individuals."

Tyagi, Pooja, Tamarra James-Todd, Lidia Mínguez-Alarcón, Jennifer B Ford, Myra Keller, John Petrozza, Antonia M Calafat, et al. 2021. "Identifying Windows of Susceptibility to Endocrine Disrupting Chemicals in Relation to Gestational Weight Gain Among Pregnant Women Attending a Fertility Clinic." *Environmental Research* 194: 110638.

Vandenbroucke, Jan P, Alex Broadbent, and Neil Pearce. 2016. "Causality and Causal Inference in Epidemiology: The Need for a Pluralistic Approach." *International Journal of Epidemiology* 45 (6): 1776–86.

Vermeulen, Roel, Emma L Schymanski, Albert-László Barabási, and Gary W Miller. 2020. "The Exposome and Health: Where Chemistry Meets Biology." *Science* 367 (6476): 392–96.

Vriens, Annette, Tim S Nawrot, Willy Baeyens, Elly Den Hond, Liesbeth Bruckers, Adrian Covaci, Kim Croes, et al. 2017. "Neonatal Exposure to Environmental Pollutants and Placental Mitochondrial DNA Content: A Multi-Pollutant Approach." *Environment International* 106: 60–68.

Wang, A, KL Devick, JF Bobbs, A Navas-Acien, BA Coull, and L Valeri. 2020. "BKMR-CMA: A Novel r Command for Mediation Analysis in Environmental Mixture Studies." In *ISEE Conference Abstracts*. Vol. 2020. 1.

Webster, Thomas F, and Marc G Weisskopf. 2020. "Epidemiology of Exposure to Mixtures: We Cant Be Casual about Causality When Using or Testing Methods." *arXiv Preprint arXiv:2007.01370.*

Weisskopf, Marc G, Ryan M Seals, and Thomas F Webster. 2018. "Bias Amplification in Epidemiologic Analysis of

Exposure to Mixtures." *Environmental Health Perspectives* 126 (4): 047003.

Zheng, Yinnan, Cuilin Zhang, Marc G Weisskopf, Paige L Williams, Birgit Claus Henn, Patrick J Parsons, Christopher D Palmer, Germaine M Buck Louis, and Tamarra James-Todd. 2020. "Evaluating Associations Between Early Pregnancy Trace Elements Mixture and 2nd Trimester Gestational Glucose Levels: A Comparison of Three Statistical Approaches." *International Journal of Hygiene and Environmental Health* 224: 113446.

Zou, Hui, and Trevor Hastie. 2005. "Regularization and Variable Selection via the Elastic Net." *Journal of the Royal Statistical Society: Series B (Statistical Methodology)* 67 (2): 301–20.

Printed in Great Britain
by Amazon

75541221R00068